HOW TO CREATE
KIND SCHOOLS

of related interest

Rising Above Bullying
From Despair to Recovery
Carrie Herbert and Rosemary Hayes
Foreword by Esther Rantzen
ISBN 978 1 84905 123 1
eISBN 978 0 85700 227 3

Essential Listening Skills for Busy School Staff
What to Say When You Don't Know What to Say
Nick Luxmoore
ISBN 978 1 84905 565 9
eISBN 978 1 78450 000 9

That's So Gay!
Challenging Homophobic Bullying
Jonathan Charlesworth
ISBN 978 1 84905 461 4
eISBN 978 0 85700 837 4

Self-Harm and Eating Disorders in Schools
A Guide to Whole-School Strategies and Practical Support
Pooky Knightsmith
ISBN 978 1 84905 584 0
eISBN 978 1 78450 031 3

Helping Adolescents and Adults to Build Self-Esteem
A Photocopiable Resource Book
2nd edition
Deborah M. Plummer
ISBN 978 1 84905 425 6
eISBN 978 0 85700 794 0

The KidsKope Peer Mentoring Programme
A Therapeutic Approach to Help Children and Young
People Build Resilience and Deal with Conflict
Nina Wroe and Penny McFarlane
ISBN 978 1 84905 500 0
eISBN 978 0 85700 903 6

HOW TO CREATE
KIND SCHOOLS

12 EXTRAORDINARY PROJECTS MAKING SCHOOLS HAPPIER AND HELPING EVERY CHILD FIT IN

JENNY HULME

FOREWORD BY CLAUDE KNIGHTS,
CEO OF KIDSCAPE

Jessica Kingsley *Publishers*
London and Philadelphia

Picture credits: Anthony Horowitz © Jon Cartwright (courtesy of Walker Books);
Jill Halfpenny © Kidscape; Jamie Oliver © The Prince's Trust; David Charles
Manners © Diversity Role Model; Baroness Janet Whitaker © Friends, Families
and Travellers; Henry Winkler © Achievement for All; David Domoney © Thrive;
Jane Asher © The National Autistic Society; Linda Jasper © Brian Slater; Michael
Sheen © Carers Trust; Jack Jacobs © Beat; Ade Adepitan © Kelly Hill.

First published in 2015
by Jessica Kingsley Publishers
73 Collier Street
London N1 9BE, UK
and
400 Market Street, Suite 400
Philadelphia, PA 19106, USA

www.jkp.com

Library of Congress Cataloging in Publication Data
A CIP catalog record for this book is available from the Library of Congress

British Library Cataloguing in Publication Data
A CIP catalogue record for this book is available from the British Library

ISBN 978 1 84905 591 8
eISBN 978 1 78450 157 0

Printed and bound by Bell and Bain Ltd, Glasgow

Contents

Foreword

Kidscape was launched 30 years ago, the first charity in the UK to really examine the culture of school bullying. It remains at the forefront of new techniques and support, and brings its wealth of expertise to consultations with the government on issues affecting children, to teacher training, to the media and to the thousands of parents and children who contact the charity each year.

Kidscape sees the phenomenal work schools do every day to protect the children in their care. It has, though, learned with and from teachers that the culture of the classroom and playground can create an environment where bullying still exists and even thrives. Teachers know better than anyone that children need to feel safe and happy if they are going to learn and so fulfil their potential, and they also know how bullying can sabotage that. They understand how it can have a devastating impact on those feelings of security and happiness, and on children's learning and results.

This book asks some pertinent questions – why do children bully, why does a culture of bullying still exist, and what can be done about it? It sees Kidscape bringing together a whole group of different charities, each with their own specific aims and objectives, but who all – at the end of the day – are trying to answer those questions and share the single hope of ensuring that no child goes into or comes home from school feeling scared, isolated or excluded. And it visits schools across the UK working with those charities to create safer, happier and more inclusive settings. The schools have some great stories to tell, about how it is sometimes the simplest ideas, and the smallest shifts in attitude, which can have the most marvellous effect – enriching not only the life of the child who has struggled to fit in, but also the life of every child in their class. These stories show us how children – when given the skills, support, setting and opportunity – can be a force for change, the school's most powerful tool in tackling bullying and creating kinder schools. What better way to celebrate Kidscape's anniversary than to share these stories with you.

Claude Knights, CEO, Kidscape

Acknowledgements

I am so grateful to all the schools and charities, parents and students who shared their experiences and expertise with me during the writing of this book, and to the charity ambassadors who spoke to me about the issues and charities close to their heart. I am indebted to Peter Bradley and the team at Kidscape for helping me bring this publication to life. My thanks, too, to my editors at JKP, to Ian Whybrow, Ali Filder, Liz Eddowes and Vanessa Greatorex for their support, and to Mark Blayney for all the wise words and advice. This is for all the children who want and so deserve to fit in and be happy at school, for my parents who taught me how much kindness matters, and for my own children (pictured here, with the wonderful Henry Winkler) who inspired and helped me to write this book.

Jenny Hulme

Introduction

What Makes a Kinder School?

'A school where everyone feels valued – where there is
a more equitable balance of power – benefits everyone,
including the bullies and the bystanders.'

PETER BRADLEY, DIRECTOR OF SERVICES, KIDSCAPE

Every month you will read about a young person, or more than one, who has taken their life as a result of being bullied. And for every suicide there are dozens of failed attempts. The Carers Trust reports that over half of school-age carers in the UK (and it suggests there may be 700,000) are bullied. The National Autistic Society says that over 700,000 children have autism (70% are taught in mainstream settings), and at least four out of ten are bullied. The Children's Society says that 63 per cent of young Travellers have been bullied or attacked, and Diversity Role Models (DRM) reports a shocking rise in homophobic bullying. According to one survey, some 66 per cent of LGBT (lesbian, gay, bisexual and transgender) students suffer bullying at school, and half of them skip classes as a result. Many more charities direct their resources to picking up the pieces once children have left school without either the results or self-worth they need to progress, and they know that bullying features frequently in their stories.

None of these figures can simply be blamed on life at school. Kidscape knows that teachers are doing an amazing job, sometimes in the most difficult of circumstances. They see the evidence of that when they go into schools. But few teachers Kidscape speaks to deny bullying still exists or the problems it still causes for too many children (and schools and parents that do deny the problem are – says Kidscape – the ones that worry them most). Schools tell the charity they know the aforementioned figures are a real and clear symptom of a need for change – in attitudes and actions – and that none of the change can happen without clear leadership from the top.

As Kidscape celebrates its 30th anniversary, it believes that there has never been a better time to explore how we can all help create kinder schools. Many of the teachers and charities and parents featured in the stories that follow would like to throw this issue into the ring as the country (political parties, teaching unions, the media and more) discusses what the future of education should look like, what we really want it to achieve, and how we can measure just how successful it has been. So those same charities, teachers and parents are inviting us to look at the power of the young peer mentor, meeting and welcoming his classmate who struggles to leave his mum and get to school in the morning; the grandmother from a family of Gypsies who is coming into school to help with a history class; the autism awareness workshop for every child in a mainstream comprehensive; the Buddy bench so children can always find a pal to play with at break times; the gay role model smashing stereotypes and helping children understand how damaging gay banter can be; the dance class for children at risk of exclusion; and the school caretaker digging over the plot with the child who can't always face his class but who comes into school each day – and learns his lessons – because he loves to garden…

While no one project pretends to offer a panacea for all the ills of school behaviour, the schools who have adopted them are seeing that the kindness and inclusivity they encourage can, actually, help them make a difference to the bullying statistics, and at the same time, meet many of the targets (attendance, behaviour, health, and academic results) when many other policies they have in place seem to be failing to produce the goods.

'What seems clear is that sometimes there is too heavy a focus on teaching subjects, rather than teaching children,' says Peter Bradley, Kidscape's director of services, who has been working with the charity since 2009. 'As well as encouraging and supporting academic achievement, one of the principle roles of education is, surely, creating happy individuals who'll become good citizens who add something to the community in which they live.

'We're seeing that if you teach children, not only about differences and specific needs, but also how to be aware of their emotions, in control of them, and how to interact with others, they will actually learn the academic subjects better, faster and more effectively at the same time,' says Peter. 'We need to stop feeding the myth that being badly treated at school toughens you up for the big bad world outside. That "big world" not only has more legislation to protect people from discrimination than a school does, but it is looking for strong team players – good citizens as well as good exam results. And if you look at any of those "top 100" listings of UK companies, you'll see they are being judged not only on their profits but on the health, wellbeing and happiness of the people who work there.'

What is your anti-bullying policy doing to help?

Peter Bradley fears that in too many schools, any anti-bullying policy is filed away for the next Ofsted inspection rather than being a document that is delivered to and agreed by the staff, and lived out in the way the school operates.

'In the teacher training workshops we run, we can split a single school's staff into nine groups to discuss a bullying scenario, and we'll hear nine different opinions about what the child's need was, whether the behaviour towards them was bullying, and how the school should react,' says Peter. 'That is a clear indication of how unfamiliar teachers are with the anti-bullying policy, or how unclear it is.' He suggests that the multi-faceted nature of bullying is one of the stumbling blocks in creating clear policies and kinder schools. 'Many schools and their students argue that playground banter (be it the "you're so gay" or "you're so weird") or persistent one-way teasing (about hair colour, clothes, the inability to catch or kick a ball) or even the repeated tripping up and pushing over of one of the class, is part and parcel of school life and it's the children on the end of it who could do with becoming more resilient so they're ready for the real world.

'But we know that bullying behaviour like this does not serve that purpose – does not, in fact, serve *any* positive purpose,' says Peter. 'The only clear evidence is that bullying has powerful negative effects that can last a lifetime. It is something quite different that builds resilience.

'We're not unrealistic about the reality of school life,' he insists. 'Some negative interactions are inevitable and can even be useful. It's a bit like stress. A modicum of stress is good for you, and helps you focus and achieve. But too much, and you are unable to cope and are no longer productive. Some low level of fallings-out can be useful in helping a child better negotiate exchanges and friendship in the future, but that has to happen in the right environment, with the right support,' says Peter.

'But no one could think that someone who feels isolated and unhappy, or whose every other interaction in the playground is negative, is going to learn anything useful, at that moment or when they get back into class. There might be days when they are not picked on (a fact often cited by teachers, as if in the school's defence), but if those children are constantly scared of bullying, and what might happen next – and with good reason – the fear is real, and that is completely unacceptable.

'All our interactions can shape our view of the world and our place in it. A culture of bullying in school, when left unchecked, creates a reality for some children where they shape a view of themselves as worthless and the world around them as something that is not safe and cannot be trusted.'

Helping the bully – and the bystanders

Kidscape also believes schools too often see anti-bullying initiatives as serving the purpose of those children on the margins – the ones who are bullied – when, in fact, they can also support and help the bully – help everyone in the school – by shifting the culture in both the classroom and the playground.

'We know it isn't good to hurt others with words or physical violence. What most children need – what we all need – is to know what the boundaries of acceptable behaviour are: this far, no further. Otherwise we are always trying to find out where the boundaries lie. What starts as "you can't play" becomes "you can't play because everyone hates you" and so on. We hear teachers say the bullied child has to learn to ignore mean children, or toughen up, but if the "bully" is never taught to think about what they are doing, but rather is able to get away with being top dog and ruling the school roost, what will it feel like when that doesn't happen? If they never learn their limitations, they will never know how to deal equally with failure and success, or understand healthy interactions between themselves and others and that can – when they finally leave school – impact on their own ability to hold down a job or have a successful relationship.

'And what is happening to all those looking on,' asks Peter. 'We know that the children who stand and do nothing – the bystanders – hurt a bullied child by their inactions. And what are they learning about their own power to do the right thing? Or the support that will be offered by their teachers and peers if they ever need help, or are feeling isolated or scared?

'We hear too often about playground cultures of leaders and followers, populars and unpopulars from children who visit us. That culture feeds an imbalance where bullying can thrive and where bystanders are encouraged to stay silent. Often teachers we talk to have suddenly recognised that children who appear confident, popular, apparent leaders, have crossed the line into the area where they are manipulative and aggressive and controlling,' says Peter. 'Teachers know that they are not doing any child any favours ignoring that. Children need to learn empathy, and how to care for others. They might say the right things in class, but they have to show they have learned it in the way they behave outside the class. This learning is crucial to them finding their place in society. A school where everyone feels valued – where there is a more equitable balance of power – benefits everyone, including the bullies and the bystanders.'

Celebrating difference: why your head teacher can change the world

What marks out the projects in this book (and there are, of course, scores more besides) is first, their recognition that schools are made up of individuals who develop and learn in different ways, and second, their ongoing and very active search for a better understanding of those individual children in their care (be it through their parents, carers, relevant charities and experts, or by more focused observation in class). So rather than a child with needs being made to feel grateful for their place at the school, but then being left on the sidelines of the class, or rather than seeing inclusion as an exercise in getting the child to fit in with their peers and with the school – the one-size-should-fit-all mentality – they are changing something at the school to ensure it fits with the child, with all children, whatever their developmental or individual differences. They are ensuring that every child becomes part of the student body – having a life and a laugh and learning alongside a peer group that understands and values them.

'The key point – and the great thing – is that none of this is rocket science,' says Neil Humphrey, professor of psychology of education at the University of Manchester. 'The big shift needs to be in attitudes, and that can be the biggest challenge. But once you've shifted attitudes, the practical things are really straightforward, and some could be introduced next week into schools.'

Those practical things include supervised lunchtime clubs where children can have fun and feel valued and safe, or it might be a policy of letting children with autism who find the chaos of corridors a problem leave class with appointed friends two minutes ahead of the bell so they can get to the next class two minutes earlier. It might involve recruiting a peer mentor for a child who finds it hard to fit into a social group, or allowing a young carer extra time with their work, or permission to arrive late.

'But still, it's a resistance to change that is sometimes the issue,' says Neil.

Some charities and schools suggest that resistance comes from those who want to defend society's – and their school's – status quo, those who don't really want to share the wealth of social inclusion and who, if they are honest, are themselves slightly fearful of those who are different, because of disability or ethnic or social background or sexual orientation, and who want to resist those children becoming the norm, taking away attention from the 'normal' majority. It is, of course, attitudes like this that have fed inequality for generations.

Neil Humphrey suggests that sometimes – hopefully more often – it is simply because people struggle to understand a social issue or disability, especially if that same child looks okay and appears to be managing the academic work. 'People – students and teachers – can simply struggle to empathise and understand when this child's experience of the world is so different from theirs,' he says.

The projects described in this book simply aim to improve that understanding among teachers, parents and students. They are helping children to empathise with their peers, and to think about what kind of human beings they would like to be, what kind of society they want to live in – or one day want their own child to live in, whatever their ability or difference or disability. Without exception, they are led from the top by head teachers who say they aren't willing to compromise their beliefs on what education is all about in order to get that league table place – head teachers who are working *with* families who face barriers to learning, rather than blaming those families for the problems in schools; head teachers who are listening to both a gut feeling that their school can be a better, kinder place and to outside experts who are helping them find out how; head teachers who say they judge their own success, and the school's success, not on overall results, but on the success and happiness of their most vulnerable student.

'These are all examples of school leaders who are utilising education as their most powerful tool – teaching every member of staff as well as the students about differences, and creating a culture where they could be accommodated, supported and celebrated,' says Peter Bradley. 'By cutting through stereotypes and by giving both staff and children the facts (about life with autism, or life as a carer, or life as a Gypsy, or life with dyslexia) and the space (via an organised club, alternative training or peer mentoring) to understand those children who are different or who are struggling, they have created platforms in their schools where students can get to know each other in the truest sense.'

Creating a better classroom culture for everyone

The schools mentioned in this book don't pretend to be perfect – indeed, head teachers see their efforts as work in progress. But there is something different about them. Children who previously might have been left on the edge of the playground, feeling vulnerable and so getting picked on, and being told they are 'bringing on the bullying themselves' are, through these initiatives, being given the support, focus and friendships they need to thrive, and that, in turn, seems to change the mood for everyone else. Children who previously might have been left on the margins with other marginalised young people, desperate for friendship and doing anything to get it, are being welcomed back into the fold of their class, and invited to join them out of school too. Suddenly the bullies who felt a need to assert their power over their classmates – who needed to flex their muscles in a culture of populars and unpopulars, achievers and underachievers – are finding themselves in a happier, more supportive place, with the chance to become more emotionally aware rather than taking out their frustrations on those around them.

In each and every case, these initiatives are showing that children, far from inevitably forming exclusive cliques, or worse, being prone to bullying their peers, are wonderfully receptive and willing to learn. Schools have shown that when young people are encouraged and taught how to make very human connections with their peers – both in and out of the classroom – it not only changes the life of the student they help and get to know, it changes and enriches their own life as well. It draws out the very best in children, making it clever and cool to be kind and creating a generation of ambassadors for tolerance and diversity. It also shines a light on the worst and most destructive side of human nature – the bullying, unkind and excluding side – and helps those who have fallen into that trap, for whatever reason, climb out of it.

1

Kidscape's ZAP Workshop
Time to Change Children's Lives

'We make it clear at the outset that what is happening to them is wrong, not their fault and that they all have something wonderful to offer the world.'

LINDA DAVIES, ZAP ANTI-BULLYING TRAINER

In a small hall in Central London, 15 boys and girls – all aged 11, 12 or 13 – are meeting for the first time. From senior schools across the UK, they appear a natural, normal mix of children as they tell each other about themselves.

'I'm Janey. I love fashion.'

'I'm Simon, and a bit of a geek actually. I love taking apart and rebuilding computers.'

'I'm Debbie. I love dogs. We have three.'

An uninformed observer might wonder why any one of them ended up here until, on closer inspection, they notice many hoods stay up, hands stay clenched, heads stay down and eyes flicker anxiously as they watch each other speak. For each and every one of these smart, beautiful children has been so severely bullied by their peers at their schools that they are all at risk of mental health issues, or already dealing with them. Some of the girls are self-harming, and one has stopped eating properly. Parents are reporting depression, anxiety, and one boy has already attempted suicide. Another student – immediately a favourite with this group for his super-warm smile and willing nature when they start to volunteer for role-play – has attempted to bleach his skin as a result of continual racist assaults.

These children are not only the victims of bullies, the pack mentality in their class, but also victims of a catastrophic failure of their schools' anti-bullying policies and often a complete breakdown in the relationship between teacher and parent. They are here in London to learn how to change that through what Kidscape calls its 'ZAP workshop'. While their parents and carers sit in a room downstairs sharing stories and spilling tears, and learning what else they can do to support their children, these youngsters are going to be given a lesson in self-belief and a collection of life skills – possibly life-saving skills – to help them be more assertive so they can ward off the children they are so afraid of facing in school tomorrow.

There are 15 here today, 15 more like them every two weeks, and many more on the waiting list, some for the more experiential residential courses Kidscape runs in school holidays. But the charity knows they are just the tip of the iceberg.

'Lots of the families we see here have the confidence to question the school. They can see their child's learning suffering – no child can properly focus in class when they are this unhappy – and they know that when nothing is being done to stop the problem they need to turn elsewhere for help,' says today's group leader, Linda Davies. 'But we know so many more blame themselves, thinking they are the only parents who are struggling and that they have somehow brought this on themselves. Then there are those parents who are led to believe that it is their child who is to blame – their personality or difference or idiosyncrasy somehow causing negative behaviour, which can cause all sorts of problems in the family.'

Linda is an ex-teacher turned Kidscape anti-bullying trainer. She has talked to parents and knows some of the issues they suspect are behind the bullying. She seems used to seeing children with autism, dyslexia, dyspraxia and attention deficit disorder, the exceptionally gifted or just those who feel and think of themselves as different. And then there are those who – based on endless horrible taunting – have suggested that a dislike of sport, a love of dancing, their gay parents, their skin colour or size might be part of the problem, something that somehow has made them a target for their peers.

Kidscape opened its doors in the UK in 1985, the first charity really to examine the culture of school bullying. It has done a phenomenal amount of work since, training teachers, shaping education policies and reaching tens of thousands of children with the message that they don't deserve to be bullied, and that they can do something to help make it stop.

Redressing the imbalance of power in the playground

The charity knows that bullying thrives where there is an imbalance of power, where one individual or a group of individuals exerts their feeling of superiority over those who are perceived as weaker or vulnerable. It knows, too, about the bystander effect – how children, when in a group, are less likely to do 'the right thing' than when they are on their own or with their family. With only a day with these children at ZAP, Kidscape's aim is to help them redress that imbalance by giving them back their self-belief, and an understanding of why children bully (Linda explains to the group that bullies may be insecure, spoilt, under pressure to succeed, be bullied or neglected at home), why others who they considered friends stand by and let it happen (she explains the 'bystander effect' and how, if a teacher is not helping, those children are often simply scared they'll be left on the sharp end of bullying behaviour if they challenge what's happening), and crucially, why bullies are drawn to children like those sitting in the circle today – and how they can learn to be more assertive and so prevent or avoid the verbal or physical assaults when they get back into school.

Linda has told the parents, grandparents and carers who have come to London today – some equally anxious-looking as they leave their child in this new group of strangers – that she will care for them all like her own newborn, and she does. 'We make it clear at the outset that what is happening to them is wrong, not their fault and that they all have something wonderful to offer the world,' says Linda. If they have been told they are too sensitive to bullying behaviour, she reminds them that their school – and the wider world – needs people who are sensitive, and that she is already seeing, in their exchanges, the wonderful gifts they have to offer. A few hoods have already come down.

Although these sessions are free to parents, they cost the charity hundreds of pounds per child. Kidscape's research, however, shows that more than 90 per cent of the children report returning to school and seeing a decline in the bullying that drove them to the workshop, as a result of learned and practised skills and, perhaps, this new realisation that they are not wrong, not alone, and now have this ready-made new peer support group who want to help each other get through this shared nightmare.

Linda stands up now, mimicking the body language of a bullied child at school, and asks how the group see her. 'Scared'...'shy'...'afraid' the children volunteer, nervously at first. She gently encourages them to advise how she might look more confident. 'Stand up straight,' they suggest. 'Drop your shoulders.' 'Stop fiddling with your hands...' shouts out the youngest of the group. 'Look at me...' says another.

'Brilliant,' says Linda. 'Look at them straight in the eye,' she tells them, illustrating the power of eye contact by looking at everyone in the circle in turn, straight in the eye, until they are forced to look away, defeated. 'See!' she says. 'Look at what you can do to the bully!' She moves on to using her voice to ward off unwanted attention, showing how to negotiate the path between scared and angry, both likely to attract unwanted responses from bullies and teachers alike.

Arming children with skills and confidence – and peer support

The children then practise saying 'no' – to the child who wants to take their lunch, who calls them stupid, who tells them to move away because no one likes them. Her tactics include advice on dealing with the really frightening physical assaults – thinking about where to stand in the playground so as not to be trapped, and how to make a quick exit if they feel threatened. The advice seems extreme given the age of the children, but the way they focus, their minds almost visibly whirring as they apply what Linda says to situations they know only too well, underlines how real that threat feels. In one scenario, where Linda pretends some children are after her new mobile phone, she throws it across the room, reminding the children that they are far more precious than any new smart gadget and, if it comes to it, the phone has to go. The children look at each other agreeing, the tension in their shoulders, and fearful, flickering eyes, calming slowly as they realise that everyone in the room recognises these scenarios as well as they do. As they realise that they are all alike, and that they are understood, and among friends – a shockingly new feeling for many of them. By the time they have split into smaller groups to act out scenarios in the playground, one child playing the bullied while the others play out the verbal attack, they are effectively putting what they have learned into action, debating and playing out possible responses to the abuse they're getting every day.

'Look at you, ugly. You must be anorexic, loser.'

'What an odd thing to say to someone who's just had a Big Mac,' the girl replies with a shrug. 'And anyway, for your information I quite like the way I look.' She turns and walks away. The group claps.

'Hey, curry house,' says one small boy to his new friend who has earned this nickname in school as a result of his ethnic background. 'Yeah, mate. I love curry. Want me to cook you one? It's my forte,' says the boy in reply. They hug and return to their seat.

'You're so gay, and such a geek. Do you know we're going to get you later?' say a group of boys, nervous at even acting out such a cruel assault on their new pal. The boy stands tall and looks right at the group. 'I'm not actually gay, or a geek' he says. And then with a smile: 'I'm happy being me. But whatever…'

'In these sessions we know the children are more often than not going back into schools where bullies might be thriving and – if that is happening – bystanders believe they're powerless,' explains Linda as the groups practise their next role-play. 'So it's very much about helping them deal with the bully, who will have found their weak spot. When these children feel beaten, the bully has all the power. We want to get them to rebuff their attacker by showing they are not scared, and that they are not to be messed with. Some parents try and do that themselves by giving children lessons in self-defence, but we know that when children hit back they usually end up getting into trouble and aggravating a sense that they are somehow the one with the problem.'

In another session that Linda calls 'fogging', she sets out to prevent the children freezing when the bully attacks, and to provide ways to avoid showing their pain and hurt and frustration. She explains to the group that sometimes their responses to bullying not only provide the bully with more ammunition and footholds as they try to become more dominant, but create the impression among others (including teachers) that they, the victim, are equally mean. 'So if a bully continually mocks your spectacles or clothes or family, instead of thinking you'll shut them up by mocking them right back, aim to come back with a more creative retort,' she says.

After five minutes of debate as the children share ideas, Linda, on cue, moves towards a child with a verbal assault, inviting the creative comeback.

'You smell horrible again,' she jeers.
'I know – it's my dad's most expensive aftershave,' says one 11-year-old. There are whoops of approval.

'You look ridiculous in those clothes,' she suggests to one girl.
'I guess you won't be asking to borrow them then,' says her 'victim' with a smile.
Pats on the back then…

Lessons move on to relaxation – designed to help the children release tension when they finally get home from school rather than letting it sabotage relationships and their evenings. Lying on the floor, eyes closed, practising breathing techniques, two boys open their eyes and look right at each other and smile, giving each other a quick thumbs up. It looks as if this is working.

Later, downstairs, while Linda continues role-play practice with the children, Peter Bradley, Kidscape's director of services and a ZAP trainer, tells the parents how wonderful the group is. He is used to seeing parents waiting to hear their children's faults, a result of all those school meetings where they've been told what they or their child are apparently doing wrong, how they're somehow triggering this terrible bullying behaviour. There is an audible sigh of relief as he articulates their experience: the awfulness of seeing your child picked on for being too tall or too small, or being good at dancing but rubbish at football, for being too bright, too awkward, too soft, too kind, too different. There is an instant group nod of recognition when he talks about meetings with teachers where they might have cried and then been left to feel that it is no wonder their child is sensitive when they are so tearful – or they may have shouted, and been left to feel that it is no wonder their child has problems if they are so aggressive. He asks how many have listened to suggestions that their child needs to toughen up to deal better with school life (most nod), and how many have been called to the school when their child finally lost it and lashed out – and then been left wondering why their own reports of repeated verbal abuse went unheeded before their own child finally lost their temper. More nods now, relief that they are not the only ones…

Empowering parents to make a change

Peter tells the parents how brave they are, and that their recognition that they need help to solve the problem has already made a difference. He spells out what bullying is, clearing up in parents' minds the confusing messages many have had from schools. He confirms that when their child is being repeatedly teased or ridiculed for their abilities or looks or hair colour and are never finding it funny, they are being bullied. If children are spreading rumours, hiding their things, or they are being coerced to give away their lunch or their money, they are not weak – they are being bullied. When they are being repeatedly and purposely excluded from groups and left isolated in the playground, they are not 'not fitting in' – they are being bullied. When they are being sent abusive texts or online messages, they should not just ignore them – they should report this because it's bullying. Peter is clear that this is not acceptable behaviour, and that to be told that it is your child's fault because they are too sensitive is also not acceptable. There is, he says, no evidence at all to say living through bullying brings any benefits to anyone.

Next Peter spells out the duty of care schools have – to tackle bullying and to support children so they can feel safe and happy, and so they can learn. He suggests many parents in the room may have cried, pleaded for help, or tried to be understanding about the cause of the bullying. Parents look at each acknowledging that this is exactly what they have done. Some talk about trying to befriend the bully, say, by asking them over for tea or to hang out at the weekend, or about how they've pleaded for other parents' support, and then felt devastated when none came. Peter then explains how hard it is for parents in schools where bullying is tolerated to speak out, knowing they, too, might be seen as trouble-makers or their child ostracised by other parents and children. Sometimes, he suggests, some of the other parents might actually feel that if their own children are happy and the school is running according to rules that suit them, they are never going to rock that boat. He describes how, far from hearing about the stereotypical comic book bully in the workshops, Kidscape more often hears children describing life at the hands of the confident, popular children who roam around in close-knit and bullying groups. He explains how, when Kidscape works with schools, it encourages teachers to look harder at what happens when those popular, confident children leave the class. How, in a culture of power play, there can be a fine line between leadership and manipulation, popularity and oppression. How some children might be seen to have loads of friends, but that schools are doing no one any favours letting their oppressive behaviour thrive unchecked. Those children can fast become bullies, demanding loyalty from those in their group who, in turn, become effective bystanders, watching nervously as others are ostracised or picked on. Peter explains that in the same way it is sometimes easier for the teacher (not always consciously) to blame the weaker children, and to lay the problem at the door of the now vulnerable parents who are so willing to do anything to prevent the bullying, rather than challenge the more vocal, confident parents about their own children's behaviour.

As well as reassuring the parents that what they have felt and the way they have reacted is perfectly natural and understandable, Peter and the Kidscape team want to teach them to get more out of the school, to stop appealing to other parents for help, and to take their concerns to the top. They want parents to understand that schools do not always understand what bullying is, and, overwhelmed by the work they have to do, they may not have even read the anti-bullying policy. They may, he suggests, have only had a few hours of teacher training on the subject, and even less on any specific need a particular child presents. Too many teachers, he says, think they understand one dyslexic child or one child with autism based on one other they have taught previously when, in fact, every child with a learning challenge can present differently and have different needs. He says it is understandable that teachers don't feel they have time to seek outside help – from the parents or relevant experts – to support children more effectively, but that doesn't mean it is okay. It is not, he says, okay at all.

Then Peter arms them with skills – the ones the children have been learning so they can practise at home (absolutely vital, he says, if they are to work), and skills of their own too: knowledge of what they should expect from an anti-bullying policy, who they should speak to about it (the head and the child's teacher), suggestions as to how to log bullying, minute meetings, set dates for reviews, keep a copy of letters sent and to ask for explanations when their child's progress is not as expected. He explains how to ask the schools to advise on ways in which peer behaviour (now based on the filed records of bullying) might be having an impact on their child's progress. Like their children upstairs, the parents are relaxing now, sitting up straight, making notes, feeling empowered to make a change.

As parents leave and the team wraps up the sessions, children and parents hug each other, and then hug their new friends, who leave armed not only with skills but phone numbers and emails of their new pals who – like them – want a better life tomorrow, and who – like them – want to support each other as they go home and back into school to try to get it.

WHAT CAN KIDSCAPE DO FOR YOU?

As well as its ZAP anti-bullying workshops for children and young people, Kidscape offers a range of bespoke courses for teachers, parents and children that can be adapted to suit your needs or setting, and cover everything from assertiveness skills for children through to reviews of anti-bullying policies for head teachers. Kidscape also offers CPD (continuing professional development) accredited courses that can be delivered at their offices in London, or in a setting of your choice across most areas within the UK. Protecting children from harm is a legal requirement for schools, and one that greatly relies on staff remaining up to date on the issues within the child safeguarding arena. That is why Kidscape's courses are continually adapted to the evolving habits and behaviour of children and young people. The charity delivers training to over 7000 professionals each year, and if you'd like to find out more, visit www.kidscape.org.uk.

IN MY VIEW – ANTHONY HOROWITZ

'The truth is that bullying doesn't do anything useful for
the bully or the bullied. No good comes out of it.'

ANTHONY HOROWITZ, OBE, IS AN AUTHOR AND PATRON OF KIDSCAPE.

As a writer, I'm aware that words can be very powerful...and they can
be very harmful too. I was bullied at school when I was 12 because
I was overweight and bad at sport and the strange thing is that even
now, all these years later, I can vividly remember the experience and
can't even bring myself to write down the names I was called. They
still hurt. And the flip side was that I then lashed out with my fists –
and what did that make me? Suddenly I was the bully and I was the
one in trouble.

We all know that children have something of a pack mentality. They
want to be part of the 'in crowd' and too often that means behaving
in the same way, however unpleasant that behaviour is. The 'in' crowd
picks on someone because they're different, because of something that
sets them apart, and as I know from my own experience, that can
be brutal.

Not surprisingly, perhaps, schools are often more reactive to physical rather than to verbal attacks. But this ignores the fact that the worst bullying is the emotional kind. Children who come to Kidscape tell us this over and over again.

I don't think many adults understand how hurtful and damaging bullying can be. Even now, there are still parents and teachers who believe – incredibly – that it's a natural part of growing up, and that we should simply live with it. I have a feeling that, in the early sixties, my parents thought it might make me more of a man. A stiff upper lip and all that.

The truth is that bullying doesn't do anything useful for the bully or the bullied. No good comes out of it. There is nothing beneficial and nothing character building about it. Positive experiences, positive peer groups and positive reinforcement are what build a strong character. Not being hurt or afraid or isolated. Not hurting or causing fear.

Children often ask me if I have my old bullies in mind when I write my books, and the fact is that, yes, Alex Rider has vanquished one or two unsavoury characters drawn from my past. I still remember escaping into the library when I was at school, losing myself in the stories I found there. I wanted to be Hal or Roger in the Willard Price adventure series. Or Tintin, travelling the world. That was when I started writing stories too.

I was lucky, but I know that today many children leave school with their self-esteem in tatters as a result of what has happened there. The damage has been done.

That's why I support Kidscape. This small, incredibly hard-working charity uses highly focused methods to address the problem of bullying at an early stage. And they are extraordinarily effective. They help so many children who are bullied, and who are being damaged by bullying – not least by helping them see it's not their fault, and they're not alone. At its ZAP workshops Kidscape gives children and their parents the words and the confidence they need to bring about positive change.

It's marvellous to watch.

2

The Peer Mentor

Introducing the Best Buddy in the School World

'These children have all been sad or worried or lonely… What this scheme has done is help us create a space where they can put those feelings to good use – learn how to support each other effectively, and so build their own resilience and the resilience of the children they help.'

LIZ TURNER, TEACHING ASSISTANT, COLGATE PRIMARY SCHOOL, HORSHAM, WEST SUSSEX

As parents and children pour through the gates at Colgate Primary School on a wet Monday morning, three ten-year-old boys are standing at the door, clearly waiting for someone to arrive. They have huge smiles on their faces and lanyards round their necks, indicating that they're peer mentors, on duty today at the school gate. Anyone who thought this might be a big job for these youngsters should watch and wonder.

First a nervous-looking boy arrives, holding his mum's hand very tightly.

'It's our first day here,' explains the mum. 'We're new to the area.'

Immediately one of the boys – an even bigger smile now – gives the younger chap, Will, a gentle high-five, and then leads him and his mum through to reception where, within five minutes, mum's hand has been swapped for the mentor's and the two boys, deep in some conversation, are on their way to class.

The other two Year 6 boys are, meanwhile, welcoming their charge, this time a potential school refuser called Joe who has some learning challenges and has struggled to make friends and settle in his class group, resulting in frequent late and rather stressful arrivals after his parents have struggled to get him to school. The school suggested a mentor to help, promising Joe that if he could arrive on time he'd be met by a 'Buddy' who'd take him to his class, and who'd be there at break and lunchtime to help him make friends, or to talk to him if he was worried about school. He is in on time now every day.

This is mentoring and befriending in action, and in the now emptied reception hall of this school in Horsham, West Sussex, the way it works is displayed on a noticeboard via colourful timetables, rotas and a photo gallery of proud school 'Buddies', the title mentors have adopted at Colgate. There is a rota for Buddy lunches (mentor and mentee meet and eat at a Buddy table), a rota for the morning and lunch breaks when Buddies surf the school seeking out anyone who is lonely or work as peer mediators, sorting out squabbles so the lunchtime staff can keep their eye on the bigger picture. There's a Buddy reading and maths support session during registration, and a Buddy drop-in scheme, accessed via a box in each classroom – students can put their name or picture in the box during the week and then they're collected for some one-to-one time in the library every Tuesday afternoon. The school also has a Buddy pairing system in place for children who are regularly requesting help and who would benefit from a Buddy for a longer period. They pick their mentor from the board, where each smiling face is matched with the Buddy's list of hobbies to help children make their choice. Then, like Joe, they know they can be met each morning as they arrive, and have someone to watch out for them during the day. So powerful is this force for good, the school is now planning to take Buddies into pre-school settings to meet, play and help take away the scariness of big school for those preparing to move to primary in the following year.

Building resilience into the timetable

Colgate Primary School signed up for peer mentoring after West Sussex County Council commissioned the Mentoring and Befriending Foundation (MBF) to deliver a two-year peer support programme across 45 schools in the region, part of its Healthy Schools initiative designed to build resilience and support the emotional health and wellbeing of students. The MBF trains small teams of staff and the initial cohort of mentors in each school, and then supports them as they develop the programme and incorporate ideas to suit their setting.

At Colgate Primary School teaching assistants Liz Turner and Kerry George-Eames took the lead and decided to ask for volunteers from Year 6 to train as mentors for the rest of the 100-plus children in the school. The whole class volunteered. Now, in the second full year of the mentoring project, the trained are becoming the trainers, this morning putting the Year 5s through their paces before the current Year 6 moves on to high school.

They start with team-building exercises, each student sharing something they're good at and proud of ('cooking', 'catching', 'fishing', 'footie', 'eating food'…they volunteer). Then they have to organise themselves silently into a line by order of height to practise communicating without words, before – more noisily – forming groups of six and nominating the smallest of the group to lie on a huge piece of paper while they draw around him or her to make a body shape on their sheet.

With their poster in place they pinpoint the 'best Buddy use' of different parts of the body. Colourful crayoned arrows are soon shooting off here, there and everywhere, and they are writing down their ideas: ears to listen with, a shoulder to lean on, a nose to sniff out problems, fingers for wiping away tears, a mouth for smiling, a hand to hold, a body for support, a brain to think of a solution, feet to walk towards someone, eyes for looking out for someone, arms to comfort. There is no stopping them. There is even 'armpit hair for maturity' written on one drawing.

Before they start to role-play there is a brief debate about the issues that might come up among mentees. Hands go up and the group pitches in with potential problems: being left out of games, being teased for being slow at games, being teased for being small or big, being sad because their pet has died, being upset because their granddad is ill, feeling rubbish because they got their homework wrong…

Then they discuss the meaning of empathy.

'That means walking in another's shoes,' says one girl.

'And what about not judging, what does that mean?' asks Liz.

'That's not talking about someone behind their back,' comes the reply. 'Or guessing why they do things without asking them,' suggests another child.

Their rather astonishing ability to mix emotional understanding with practical support is then brought to bear on likely scenarios. In one corner students talk through how they'd help a younger student upset by a low mark in class, and volunteer their top three ideas: 'tell them not to worry, they've done their best; say you'll help them practise; and ask them to remember what they're good at.' Another group has been discussing how to support a student after the loss of a pet, and their top three includes: 'ask them about the good times so they remember how much fun they had with the pet; listen to them when they talk about those times; help them make a memory card.'

Creating positive playtimes

'I think we sometimes underestimate what children have to offer each other,' says Liz Turner. 'These children have all been sad or worried or lonely, and they know exactly how that feels. What this scheme has done is help us create a space where they can put those feelings to good use – learn how to support each other effectively, and so build their own resilience and the resilience of the children they help. It isn't about forcing kids to play together. It's about giving them a role and a responsibility to look after each other. It isn't about creating a playground free from problems, either. Children will be children. But this is about creating a playground where children know that the problems they come up against can and will be sorted out quickly, a playground where they can always find a friend if they run into trouble.

'We always took fall-outs and bullying seriously before,' says Liz. 'But we also know that, before, issues that seemed minor sometimes went unnoticed and undiscussed until they were much bigger, and were having a more negative effect on the child and their learning. Sometimes children were going to different adults on different days and we weren't always getting a full picture of what was going on. Because the Buddies are intervening earlier, that is not happening so much. And when problems do persist and children keep coming back to the Buddies, the Buddies talk to us. This means we can get a clearer picture of what is happening and, when necessary, intervene much earlier.'

There is, of course, the same level of adult supervision and guidance on hand in the playground, and the mentors are trained to recognise when they need to call in a grown-up. But those adults say they know they'd need to clone themselves a dozen times or more to provide anything like the support the children are providing for each other. What's more, evaluations of the scheme have shown how much more children liked talking to a Buddy about some of the problems instead of an adult, because Buddies had often had the same problem and so had a better understanding of how they were feeling. The school knows this is something that has been supported by the training of Buddies, who learn why they should never use phrases such as 'I'm very disappointed in you…' 'You've both been very silly…' 'I don't know what we're going to do with you…' and are, instead, taught to listen ('as if your life depends on it'), repeat back what they have heard ('always try to be accurate'), accept feelings ('remember that feelings are facts, so you have to accept them as real'), and help the children think forward, so they feel in charge of what happens next.

Improving learning outcomes

The MBF's programme manager for West Sussex knows that when the scheme was first presented to schools it seemed, for many, too much to think about in their already overstretched days, even though the training and evaluation was free, courtesy of the County Council. Now, however, the schools that did sign up say they wonder how they managed without it. Here, at Colgate, staff say they can start class as soon as the bell goes, instead of learning being disrupted by disputes left over from break. They have seen new children settle more quickly, fewer children being sent to the head's office, and fewer parents coming into school with concerns about their children's friendship problems. All these things have, in turn, had a positive impact on attendance, and on the work that is being done in class.

'We know that peer mentoring schemes in schools have the potential to add up to six months of learning for a child who is mentored, and we want to make that a reality here,' says deputy head teacher, Marion West, who oversees the project. 'There has to be a focus on outcomes in schools today, and we're seeing that this contributes to that process. If children are unhappy or lonely or distracted by what just happened at playtime, we know they won't focus well in class. Teachers can spend the first ten minutes of a lesson trying to deal with issues, or encouraging children to concentrate. And although the scheme is absolutely about the wellbeing of students, it's been wonderful for the wellbeing of staff too.'

MBF believe that the programme fulfils the remit of supporting children's emotional health. 'Research in this area supports the idea that intervening early to build self-esteem and resilience can protect against mental health issues in later life,' says Elaine Slater Simmons, the MBF's peer support programme manager in West Sussex. 'Research shows that half of people with existing mental health problems first experience symptoms (stress, low self-esteem, anxiety and depression) by the age of 14. At primary school level, short interactions can be enough to really make a difference,' says Elaine. 'But when children are a little older the one-to-one relationship can be especially effective.'

A high school model

One of the organisation's many success stories is a high school in Weymouth. MBF went to Budmouth technology college, a secondary school in Dorset over ten years ago and helped it develop a student-led peer mentoring scheme for the 1500 11 to 18-year-olds who study there. It was specifically aimed at those 'middle of the road' students who were not entitled to support through the special educational needs (SEN) provision, but who were struggling with confidence or transition. These were issues that the college knew could become real problems, having an impact on their attainment and leading to bullying and other behaviour problems if left alone. The programme proved such a success that it's still in place, still thriving, over ten years after MBF finished its training. Every year mentors are recruited in the spring, trained in the summer and get to work with assigned mentees (in Years 7 through to 10) as they arrive at the college in the autumn term. The principal, David Akers, is in no doubt that the scheme has helped ensure their anti-bullying policy works and works well. 'Early on we tracked 40 young people over a year, ten mentors, ten mentees, ten non-mentor students and ten non-mentored students. The improvement in attendance and behaviour for the mentors and mentored was over and above the control group,' he says. 'That success rate has continued.'

'I don't think many schools realise at the outset how much this benefits the mentor just as much as it benefits the mentee, the student he or she supports,' says Elaine. 'In an early evaluation of the programme at Colgate Primary we found 80 per cent of the Buddies had increased in self-confidence.'

'It does feel great to have helped one of the younger children,' says John, one of the current Year 6s on duty at Colgate today, and a boy who is, say teachers, one of those who finds school and making friends easy. 'I don't think I would have made friends outside my class before – I never knew Year 6s that well when I was lower down the school. It's like now this is my job I can go up to children I don't know and just ask them how they're doing. But I think the biggest difference in me is how I listen. They taught us to listen to each other rather than guessing how other students were feeling – and rather than telling them what to do or feel. I'm hoping I can be a mentor when I go to my next school as it's a great way to meet people from other years.'

Making kindness part of the everyday

'This isn't about breaking up friendship groups by taking a mentor out of them and putting them somewhere else,' says Elaine. 'It makes those friendship groups stronger by giving the mentor skills that they can take back to their own friends and with them through life. It can benefit those who are doing well at school like John, as well as those who might be struggling.'

Colgate Primary School had one boy, Simon, who was nervous of signing up, partly because he has some learning difficulties and finds social interactions difficult. 'But when we talked it through and showed him the kind of jobs he would be given to do, he agreed,' says Liz Turner. 'He's amazing with the little ones – never tires of listening to or playing with them. They love him, and he's got to know everyone in the school as a result of this scheme, and everyone in the school has got to know him. It's been a revelation.'

'I think as adults it's easy to forget how hard social issues can be, and how much they impact on our focus and happiness,' says Elaine. 'How many adults – even the most confident ones – can walk into their local pizza restaurant and enjoy eating on their own when all their peers are having a laugh at the next table? How often do we wish we could get an appointment with a doctor or counsellor to nip a problem in the bud, instead of joining a long queue and waiting to get a worry off our chest? I think what we're seeing is that these schemes give children a sense of security. They might struggle with issues but they know, if and when they do, someone is there. They'll never just be left on their own. It's creating an environment where, instead of kind acts being the ones that stand out or that pick up a house point, kind acts are part of the everyday expectation.'

'Our playground has the same issues as any playground,' says Marion West. 'The small fall-outs and same social struggles, but they don't last long, and children learn from them.'

And that is the beauty of this project. There is nothing forced about the friendships on show, and nothing getting in the way of the very natural, spontaneous games played by gaggles of friends as they pour into the playground for their break from class. Three boys are racing from one corner to the next, and two girls find a corner to make daisy chains. There are groups of children, heads together, sharing secrets. In fact it's hard at first glance to see any difference, or to pick out the six children bearing lanyards who are on playground duty today. But before too long and without warning, John from Year 6 drops the ball he's playing with, high-fives his pals, tells them he'll be back in a bit, and sets off towards a boy he's noticed emerging from the school and now standing on the sidelines on his own.

'You okay, Rob?' he says. 'Fancy a game?'

Look in a different direction and Diya is leading a child half her age and size to a quiet bench for a chat. After a few minutes she pulls out a book and starts reading to him. On the far side of the playground four eight-year-olds are being encouraged to work out what went wrong after a spat during a game. They start with hands on hips, slightly red in the face. But after a few minutes the mentor, Becky, has them laughing, and returning – together – to their game. And she is off, back to her own game and friends, job done.

Note: The names of students in this chapter have been changed.

WHAT CAN THE MENTORING AND BEFRIENDING FOUNDATION DO FOR YOU?

The Mentoring and Befriending Foundation (MBF) (previously the National Mentoring Network) is a national charity that launched over 20 years ago to help mentoring projects share good practice. Now it has a broader remit to promote befriending and mentoring, and to provide a range of services including training to help organisations increase the effectiveness and quality of their schemes.

MBF works with schools and other organisations all over the UK. Colgate Primary School's peer support programme came about after the MBF was commissioned by West Sussex County Council Public Health in 2012 to deliver the scheme in collaboration with West Sussex Healthy Schools. It is part of a strategy detailed in the West Sussex Public Health Plan 2012–17 to support people across West Sussex with their emotional health and wellbeing.

It is just one of many success stories. The MBF has had and continues to run contracts and pilot projects for a host of other government departments: Department for Education, Department for Work and Pensions, Office for Civil Society and Home Office. As well as promoting befriending and mentoring, it provides a range of services including training to help organisations increase the effectiveness and quality of their existing schemes.

MBF offers schools a range of resources (including online tools and guides starting from £10), and can help develop courses and provide in-house training to suit their setting. For more information visit www.mandbf.org/training-and-events/support-for-schools-and-colleges.

IN MY VIEW – JILL HALFPENNY

'I am a parent now so my son's happiness is my number one priority, and my heart goes out to other parents who see their children suffering in a place where they should be learning and should be happy.'

JILL HALFPENNY, TV AND STAGE ACTRESS, IS AN AMBASSADOR FOR KIDSCAPE.

No one can do their best when they are afraid. We all know that. If I go into my job fearful of what is going to happen and of the people around me, I know I won't do well. So how can children and young people who experience fear when they go into school be expected to learn effectively?

I had a taste of bullying when I was at school. When you are different, in any way or for any reason, it seems bullies like to target you. I was on a teen drama called *Byker Grove* when I was at school and was the girl who used to get picked up and taken to the studio and that triggered jealousy and bullying. Not extreme, but enough to make me miserable. Enough to make me know how important it is to support Kidscape's work now as they help families whose lives are made miserable by bullying, and as they work to promote ways to make schools kinder places to be. I am a parent now so my son's happiness is my number one priority, and my heart goes out to other parents who see their children suffering in a place where they should be learning and should be happy.

As a society we have recognised that mental and emotional bullying is just as harmful as physical. If we can accept that fact when it comes to domestic violence or verbal abuse in the workplace, we must, as intelligent adults, surely recognise the harm bullying can do in schools. Teachers transform the lives of so many children every day in thousands of classrooms around the country, and yet many still seem reticent to look harder at what is happening when those children leave the classroom. It's there – in the playground, on the bus, or when they put on their computers at home – that too many become isolated and excluded and abused.

3

The Prince's Trust xl Club
Because Everyone Deserves a Second Chance

'When students have had tough experiences growing up, it can – too
often does – lead to a tough, unkind future. A future where you are
misunderstood. The best time to change that is while they are at school.'

HELEN CABLE, TEACHER AND xl CLUB LEADER, THE
MALLING SCHOOL, WEST MALLING, KENT

Emily Hill is taking time out from her studies today to head to London following her nomination for a Pride of Britain Award. She's only 18, and seems surprised she's been nominated as an unsung hero in these annual awards – surprised by pretty much everything that's happened since her life took a turn two years ago. Back then, she was the girl no one wanted to know, and the student who teachers believed so disruptive she should be expelled.

And then there was Miss Carol Thomas.

'She was the teacher who changed things,' says Emily. 'She pretty much begged for me to be given a second chance. Just one term, she said… One term to prove I could turn things around. I think she could see that what happened to me had led to the problems I was having, but that they didn't define me. Not really.'

Emily was brought up by her grandparents in Warrington after her own mother's mental health and substance abuse problems meant she couldn't care for her. But after her mother was disabled in an accident, Emily – then only 12 – became her main carer.

'She didn't want strangers in washing and dressing her, and I liked the way she felt more comfortable with me doing those things. I thought it would bring us close, and we'd never been close,' says Emily.

Emily's mum passed away when she was 15, and the teacher – Carol Thomas – believed Emily's experience, her loss, was at the root of her anger and disruptive behaviour. Carol Thomas won her case. Emily was given a term, and it changed everything.

Carol is the teacher in charge of Emily's school's xl club, a Prince's Trust programme that works in over 500 schools and centres supporting around 8000 young people. The club takes on board students aged 13–19 who, for any number of social, emotional or developmental reasons, have ended up with critically low levels of confidence and motivation, and who are either on the brink of exclusion, or look set to fail if they stay in school. Some of the clubs even catch students once they've dropped out or been expelled, providing education in student referral units or learning centres.

The lessons they learn are part of The Trust's own bespoke but flexible curriculum that gives students a qualification, and which – more importantly – is designed to give them the confidence and self-belief they need to avoid exclusion and finish school, to move on to college or into a job. The Prince's Trust supplies the lesson plans and resources for the programme, which is designed to pretty much fit into the timetable like a GCSE. It can be condensed or expanded as schools see fit, and it allows students at the club to explore four key modules: teamwork, community involvement, enterprise skills, and the world of work.

'My nan and granddad were fed up – embarrassed really – with coming to the school for meeting after meeting about what was happening in class and, for them, the xl club was like clutching at straws in that term,' says Emily. 'But it didn't take a term for me to realise I wanted to change things, and that I could. I knew I'd been outrageous and that my appearance was terrible and that I'd stopped even caring, but suddenly I was in this group where the teachers wanted to get to know me and the students were trying to help each other. Trying to help me. It wasn't just a new group of friends, it was like a family where you had a say, a voice, a role in helping others as well as yourself. After all those meetings where I was being told what was wrong with me, it was a chance to prove that I could get some things right.

'The others on my course didn't have the same problems as me,' says Emily. 'We were a real mixed bag. Some needed help to learn. Some needed confidence. Some needed help with their behaviour. Some had been bullied. We were able to talk about what we'd been through, and they became my role models, and I became theirs. And when you did something right – like my appearance was the first thing to improve – you got praised for it. Got told they *liked* your attitude!

'It wasn't like normal school. We studied leadership, team-building, enterprise skills, cooking, beauty, mechanics, fundraising. We went on residentials and we went camping. We got to go on work placements. I worked with the Cheshire Fire Service, and when they saw how good I was with children coming in for visits and lessons on fire safety, they invited me to stay on as a volunteer. I've done my Health and Social Care Level 1, and now I'm going to college to do Level 2. I want to be a social worker – and in the meantime I've been asked to be an ambassador for The Prince's Trust. My nan and granddad couldn't be prouder.'

Emily is just one of thousands of Prince's Trust success stories, but The Trust wants to reach many thousands more like her, and it knows schools are the best place to reach them. The charity talks about that mission with a sense of urgency, and with good reason. One of its recent surveys – The Prince's Trust Macquarie Youth Index – found that more than three-quarters of a million 16–25-year-olds believe they have nothing to live for, with jobless youngsters (and there are hundreds of thousands of them) facing 'devastating' symptoms of mental health problems. The research revealed that long-term unemployed young people are more than twice as likely as their peers to believe they have nothing to live for, and to have been prescribed anti-depressants. One in three has contemplated suicide, while one in four has self-harmed. The findings were based on interviews with over 2000 16–25-year-olds, and showed that 40 per cent of jobless young people have faced these symptoms of mental health problems – including suicidal thoughts, feelings of self-loathing and panic attacks – as a direct result of unemployment.

'If you look at these figures, they are alarming,' says Paul Brown, The Prince's Trust's director of programmes. 'If young people leave school with no confidence, they can fall into a downwards spiral. They become depressed, then they can't work effectively or contribute to their community, and their problems can get worse. Programmes like ours can prevent that happening, or break into that vicious circle before too much damage is done.'

School, but not as they know it

The Malling School in Kent is one of hundreds of schools that are helping The Trust make that happen. This morning there are 12 Year 9 students around a boardroom-style table poring over plans for an event to raise money for Fundway Trust, a local mental health charity, which will, at the same time, contribute to their efforts to achieve The Prince's Trust qualification, the Personal Development and Employability Skills (PDE).

They share ideas and work out who's going to do what, Raj: press, Liam: health and safety, Caz: finance, Kayleigh: publicity, before retreating behind laptops with a task to complete. Occasionally they'll call out to the teacher in charge – Helen Cable – and ask her opinion, or how to spell something, and then other students might chip in and there'll be some discussion around one of the student's ideas. There is, otherwise, silence for the next hour or so.

This is still school for these students, but not as they've known it. This time last year, most of the young people in this room couldn't concentrate – wouldn't even stay on their chairs – for more than two minutes at a time. Some were so disruptive they were, like Emily, at risk of exclusion; others had effectively disengaged with their academic life. A mixed bag of learning challenges and/or students who had become isolated and misunderstood, they all had a chronic lack of confidence.

As part of The Prince's Trust xl club qualification, the students in this group at The Malling School have already studied presentation and communication skills, event management, money management, healthy living, personal development and team-building. Helen's Year 10 xl club is in another part of the school on a road safety course.

Class-based project work is matched with practical excursions. Helen has recently taken her clubs on a trip to a magistrates' court to practise their observation skills, taken them out for pizzas so they can practise their social skills, and last week they hosted a fundraiser to practise their new teamwork and event management skills.

A student arrives late, sits down by Helen, and rolls his eyes.

'I'm done for, Miss,' he says. 'Just had an appointment with the counsellor. Missed much?'

Helen gives the 13-year-old, Shaun, a warm smile and makes room on the table so she can update him on the club's progress and discuss what role he wants to take.

'Shaun wants to work in a zoo when he's older,' says Helen. 'He's brilliant with animals and knows so much about them.'

The boy sitting next to her still looks worn out, but – relaxing a little now – looks up and starts to talk to her about the different species he's read about and would like to help protect in the future. He has no pets, and has never been to a zoo. He has, in fact, never been far out of this part of Kent where he lives with his gran, coming to a school he used to hate, with little belief in what he could achieve when he finally finished. But his ambitions now are as real and as vivid as any other child's of a similar age. Another student, Kayleigh, comes over to get some advice from Helen and to show her some photos of work she's been doing at home on her theatre make-up project: a collection of the most realistic looking scars and cuts, and the most beautiful face painting.

'You have so much talent, Kayleigh,' says Helen, looking through each one. 'Stunning.'

Expecting more of each other

'One of the things we love about the xl club is that the projects allow us to harness what our students love doing when they're not at school,' says Helen who was nominated by her school to run the xl club, and was trained and is supported by The Prince's Trust. 'Minecraft, face-painting, conservation, make-up and hair, skateboarding, fishing – loads of the lads love fishing. We can build those passions into some of the projects we're working on, and through them they learn so much more about themselves and each other, and the kind of jobs they'd like to have, and what they need to do next to make that happen. While they have to learn to work together, they can progress at their own rate. But they have expectations of each other, they need each other to be part of the team effort – and that is something many of them haven't experienced before, and it gives them motivation to move forward.'

Helen knows these students are just at the beginning of their journey, but she couldn't be prouder.

'They are great, aren't they?' she says, beaming. 'Their attention is wonderful, and school attendance is now really good. Their desire to please is really moving sometimes. I think they're as protective of me as I am of them. They want to belong to something. They want to be good at something. We did a teamwork unit which was all about acknowledging what they were good at, but also what they were not good at and how to access help to get better. We've done a lot of work on communication skills and how to give and take constructive criticism, and how that skill can help you achieve your personal goals.'

The Prince's Trust programme is no magic wand – it can take weeks, months and even several terms to turn things around – but it stems from the rather magical principle set down by the charity's own president (HRH The Prince of Wales) when it was founded in 1976, and shared, they believe, by so many teachers around the UK.

'Our president believed then, and believes now, that every young person has potential. He believes that given the chance, every young person in this country would like to do something good with their life,' says Paul Brown. 'That positive energy now runs through everything we do. It shapes scores of projects and programmes that help young people at pivotal times in their life – when they're leaving the care system, leaving (or being forced to leave) school, leaving prison, leaving gangs…'

The league table debate

Just as you won't find The Prince's Trust's xl club on the national curriculum, you won't find its success stories in the league tables. While the course is accredited – every student works towards the PDE qualification that stays on their Personal Learning Record – it doesn't count towards the school's league table results.

However, it will be helpful for anyone rating a school on its league tables position to know that while NEET statistics (not in education, employment or training) for 16- to 24-year-olds still stand at over a million in the UK (and nearly half of that million are deemed economically inactive, that is not work-ready rather than unemployed), the presence of an xl club represents a school willing to give its disengaged students a second chance to lose the negative labels, to make new friends and benefit from a positive peer experience, and to give them a real shot at getting a future they deserve. Anyone rating a school might also want to know that some 90 per cent of students in this programme show positive skill development across a range of areas during the programme, and that at the end of it nearly nine out of ten of them move on to further education or training or into a job.

This has the chance, then, to inform the ongoing debate about vocational qualifications in schools, after reforms by the coalition government cut the value of hundreds of vocational qualifications that used to count as GCSE equivalent. There are currently only 70 or so on league table lists considered to demonstrate the rigour required, and which have a record of getting people good jobs or a place at university.

The suggestion during these reforms was that many schools were steering their students towards what they considered 'easier' exams in order to bump up their league table position. The worry was – and still is – that the effective downgrading of those qualifications will lead to schools removing them from their curriculum. Even if the government didn't consider them guaranteed job-finders, these courses were undoubtedly encouraging many disengaged young people to have another go, giving many students the confidence and a sense of achievement that they weren't getting from more academic subjects, and so opening the door – opening their minds – to the possibility that they could get other qualifications and training.

Ofsted has also stressed that, as students stay in schools until the age of 18, schools have to ensure that the curriculum meets the needs of individual learners, and they gain meaningful qualifications and experience to help them achieve their career goals. Businesses, contributing to that conversation, are reminding politicians that their world needs good citizens as well as good qualifications – citizens who are humble but confident, inquisitive but resilient, and who are not just going to seek out personal success but make a difference to the company they work in, and the world around them.

'Of course we absolutely believe academic skills and qualifications are important,' says Paul Brown. 'Children do need basic literacy, numeracy and technical skills for every job. But vocational skills are just as important. They can include very applicable hard skills that can be taken into a job, and also cover teamwork, communication, customer service and more which can really make a difference when young people move into college or into work. Issues like confidence and motivation are too often seen as trivial, but they are absolutely fundamental to what young people do with their lives. When they demonstrate those skills – when they stand up and talk about what they are going to do next in front of a room full of people at one of our events – the change we witness is massive. The change is marvellous.

'We know that by giving over some of their curriculum to The Trust's xl club, students are more likely to achieve in their other studies,' says Paul. 'The progress may not be linear. They may or may not take those other GCSEs at the same time; many go on to do them when they leave school and move into college. But each week they leave the xl club feeling empowered, and by the end of the programme they have developed the belief in their own potential to get the exams they need, and to get the job they want.'

See the change – make a change

'Our head could see the potential of this and decided to introduce it into the curriculum,' says Helen Cable at The Malling School. 'Other teachers can see the evidence now. They are not only seeing the results we get at the end, but they are seeing the difference when these students go back into their other lessons, and they are seeing that difference pretty quickly.

'In a society where we promote equal opportunities, there have to be *suitable* opportunities,' says Helen. 'If the focus is on academic achievement – if that's all that counts, which is what the league tables sometimes suggest – and you tell students they are not good enough to take those exams, or you put them in for exams and they learn they are not good enough because they fail, then you risk giving them the idea they don't count, and create a self-fulfilling prophecy. And what is the sense in that?

'When students have had tough experiences growing up, it can – too often does – lead to a tough, unkind future. A future where you are misunderstood. The best time to change that is while they are at school. Our xl club opens a window on to a world that will take another look at them, and give them a second chance.'

Note: The names of The Malling School students in this chapter have been changed.

Resources

Ofsted Further Education and Skills Annual Lecture.

Ofsted (2014) 'Transforming 16–19 education and training: the early implementation of 16 to 19 study programmes.' London: Ofsted. Available at www.gov.uk.

The Prince's Trust at www.princes-trust.org.uk.

Office for National Statistics at www.ons.gov.uk/ons/index.html.

HOW CAN THE PRINCE'S TRUST HELP YOU?

The Prince's Trust was founded in 1976 by HRH The Prince of Wales and is now the UK's leading youth charity, offering a range of programmes including training, personal development, business start-up support, mentoring and advice.

The Prince's Trust xl club at The Malling School was launched in 1998 and is just one of those provided by The Trust to give young people the chance to grow and reach their potential. The clubs are suitable for 13- to 19-year-olds and are designed to be informal and flexible in their approach using relevant, experiential learning to give students qualifications and skills to aid employment. Schools can use the curriculum over the course of a term or two, or for longer periods.

The qualification offered via the xl club programme is called the Personal Development and Employability Skills (PDE), and is regulated by Ofqual in England, Wales and Northern Ireland. In Scotland it is approved by SQA (Scottish Qualifications Authority) and is called the SPDE.

If your school is interested in running a Prince's Trust programme, you can find contact numbers and advice via the learning hub at www.princes-trust.org.uk.

IN MY VIEW – JAMIE OLIVER

'At the end of the day you'll be judged on what you do,
not just on what your qualifications say. Stick to your guns,
trust your gut instincts and dare to be different...'

JAMIE OLIVER, MBE, TV PRESENTER, CHEF, AUTHOR AND
ENTREPRENEUR, IS AN AMBASSADOR FOR THE PRINCE'S TRUST.

Today's young people have so much to offer, but too often their skills
and talents are going to waste – often through lack of self-belief or
opportunity.

It's easy to worry and feel insecure about the future when you're
younger. It doesn't matter if you're not top of the class – you don't
have to be good at everything to be successful, and it certainly doesn't
mean you're thick. At the end of the day you'll be judged on what you
do, not just on what your qualifications say. Stick to your guns, trust
your gut instincts and dare to be different – while it's much easier to
go with the flow, it's good to have your own opinions and thoughts.
Speak your mind and be honest and it'll be worth it in the end. The

most important thing for young people to remember is that by simply applying themselves and finding a passion, they can go on to do wonderful things.

I'm lucky enough to do something I'm really passionate about but I have worked really, really hard to get there. When you're starting at the bottom, you have no idea that you're ever going to achieve success, but if you want something badly enough and you're willing to work very hard, you can get there.

4

The Role Model

Helping Students Smash Some Stereotypes – and Embrace Equality

'We need to open young people's eyes to other people's struggles and show them that their emotional intelligence – and empathy is a mark of that – is as important as anything else they develop at school.'

NAVAH BEKHOR, TEACHER, DIVERSITY ROLE MODELS

On a school trip a group of 15-year-olds sat round a campfire and spun a bottle and dared a dare. When it pointed at Jamie, the dare was to kiss another boy in the group. First he resisted, but as the chants of 'chicken' and 'do it, do it' got louder, he turned and planted a kiss on his classmate's lips. There was laughter, there were photographs, there were a few red faces. The dare was done. When the group returned to school, the story and photo were passed around and Jamie got landed with the label 'gay' – in class, at break, on the bus home and, before long, on social media too. The taunts got louder, nastier and the pressure grew. Jamie was soon ostracised, scared, and felt he couldn't cope. He wasn't, in fact, gay. But that wasn't the issue anymore. He was told he was gay and was made to feel worthless, dirty, and alone. When nothing was done to stop the problem, or to help him, he took his own life.

In a school a few miles outside Liverpool, a different group of 15-year-olds have their eyes closed and their heads down on their desks. They are being asked to take part in a private poll, and the teacher at the front doesn't want their votes to be influenced by their peers, or their responses to be picked up by them after the class is over.

'How many of you have used the word "gay" to describe someone's clothes or hobbies or friendships?' she asks. Hands are raised. 'How many of you think it's okay to use the word "gay" in that way?' Hands again, fewer maybe – some hesitant, taking theirs down, their minds probably changing as they are being forced to think about what they have said, perhaps for the first time. 'How many of you would feel comfortable telling your friends that you are gay?' No hands at all now.

When they open their eyes they are told Jamie's story, and are introduced to a group of visitors, 20-, 30- and 40-somethings here at the school today with the charity Diversity Role Models (DRM). Before they're properly introduced, the class is asked to hazard a guess as to which of the group has worked as a model, a football player for their country, a Buddhist, a teacher. Which of them do they think is married, a parent, and who would they guess is gay…

Like thousands of other Year 9s and 10s who are taking part in this sort of workshop, the students in this class are being challenged to own up about how they feel about lesbian, gay, bisexual and transgender (LGBT) issues, and about LGBT people who live and work alongside them. So yes, they think the 20-something male is the footie star, and maybe the woman who looks a little older with long hair is the teacher, and the smartly dressed woman is the adviser to the PM… And of course they're wrong. The smartly dressed woman is a Buddhist and gay and had, herself, attempted suicide as a result of her friends' and family's reaction to her sexuality. The woman with the long hair is, in fact, transgender and, as a schoolboy hero for Scotland's under-18s, saved a goal from Teddy Sheringham and then, when coming out about gender confusion, was often ostracised. She's also the one who has been married the longest (to her male partner of 25 years after a successful sex–change operation) and is now a consultant for the coalition government on diversity issues. All the role models have their own stories to tell, and stereotypes to smash to smithereens.

Diversity Role Models (DRM) is a relatively new UK charity, launched by teacher Suran Dickson after she became aware of the rise in homophobic bullying in schools. The charity – now with the broadcaster Clare Balding OBE as its patron – says tens of thousands of LGBT young people suffer from bullying at school, and many never report it.

But Suran knew it wasn't just a problem having an impact on students who were LGBT.

'The Teachers' Report, a major YouGov survey of primary and secondary school teachers, revealed that nearly all secondary teachers and two in five primary school teachers say students experience homophobic bullying, even if they are not gay. Teachers revealed that boys who work hard, girls who play sport, young people with gay parents, and young people who are thought to be gay, can all experience homophobic bullying,' says Suran. 'More report indirect abuse via the phrase "you're so gay" or the use of terms like dyke, queer, faggot and poof, which not only hurt the targets, but effectively promote the idea that being LGBT is something to be sneered at. Yet, according to the YouGov survey, nine in ten staff in schools say they've never received any specific training on how to prevent and respond to homophobic bullying.'

Suran was also very aware of the fact that none of the students she taught had an issue with her own sexuality, and she noticed there was far less gay banter in her class. She was gay and they knew it, but they liked, trusted and respected her. She launched DRM to introduce more children and young people to LGBT adults so they, too, could get to know the person behind the stereotype and, as they did, help her challenge the rise of homophobia in schools.

The charity knows the enormity of its task. Section 28 (the law banning any discussion of homosexuality in schools) was only overturned in 2003, and has left a long shadow over equality and diversity. In the absence of any discussion about these issues, a whole generation has learned to use 'gay' as a term of abuse, and a rising number of young people are being bullied because they are gay, because their parents are gay, or perhaps simply because the way they dress or what they do in their spare time fits with their peers' stereotypical view of what gay people do. DRM is here to undo that damage, and to make young people think again.

The banter and the bullying

The workshop in Liverpool leads on to a heated debate about whether it is okay to use the banter 'you're so gay', and students volunteer that it might be okay among friends, say, if one of them is wearing some kind of man bag, or because of the way he dances or walks. Another points out that actually, come to think of it, that when they do that it is to take the p*** out of that bag or that walk. The kids snigger, recognising the situation, recognising themselves in it. A few boys suggest the person should get over it, it's only a joke, and some girls round on them and point out that a joke is only a joke if both parties find it funny.

Navah Bekhor, a teacher herself and now the woman leading DRM's schools programme, is interested, asking if they think it's fair to take a description of someone's sexuality and use it in that way. She asks them if they are okay with people being gay, and all but two boys in the class say they are. She asks, then, why none of them would feel comfortable coming out at school. The previous poll, she says, showed that not one of them would be comfortable coming out at school. No one has an answer, but they quickly work out that part of the reason they wouldn't come out in this class is precisely because of the way this class talks about being gay.

'We always make it absolutely clear that this is not about coming out,' says Navah. 'We'd never encourage anyone to do that until they are absolutely ready. It's about making them think how their attitudes – how even gay banter among friends – are feeding stereotypes that this is something weird or wrong or something to be scoffed at. We ask them in these workshops to think about how a young person who is 13 or 14 or 15 will feel if they think they might be gay, or a member of their family is gay, when they hear that word used to denote being rubbish or abnormal. You can see the realisation on their faces. Like, "yes, that is what I have been saying" and "that is the hurt I might have caused". I was just at a school in Scotland and they'd set up all kinds of diversity groups, including (but not only) a gay/straight alliance.

'We believe most students we meet do not intend to be homophobic and wouldn't really care if their friends were straight or gay. Sadly, though, there is a very vocal minority who are homophobic. We hope the workshop will help that minority think again, but we also know that the workshops help the majority feel better equipped to deal with their homophobic remarks and bullying and so help us make a change.'

There is nothing preachy or sanctimonious about these sessions. The role models and Navah walk around the class, working with groups as they debate issues around their language and their attitudes to people who seem gay or who are gay. One group has started talking about the civil rights movement and racism, and how casual racism was so deeply damaging. They recognise that it wasn't just people who were black who were fighting for civil rights – people who were white were standing beside them. Navah asks them to think about what kind of society they want to live in now, what kind of changes they'd like to see in their future, and what kind of society their generation wants to create.

Before the students troop out, they are asked to take part in another private poll, and the results have changed. When asked if they would use the term 'gay' in a teasing or bullying way, no one says they would. Some of the students also hang back – to say sorry to the role models, and to shake their hands and wish them well.

Facing up to teachers' fears

Many schools are – have been – nervous of what DRM wants to do, and are even more nervous about what parents will say. But the teacher training the charity provides is thorough and practical and aims to give teachers the facts and therefore the confidence to answer any concerns. They work through scenarios likely to throw them – such as the student who says that being gay is disgusting and against their religion, or the parent who objects on the grounds that they don't want their child learning about sex in the classroom – and provide the answers: sensible, informed challenges to that way of thinking.

'We know sometimes when we go into schools that this issue has never even been discussed in the staff room. When we do teacher training it's surprising how many teachers stumble over the word "gay". You realise that if they're not comfortable talking about this issue with their colleagues, how will their students be able to use it maturely and comfortably? What message is that sending out?' says Navah. 'We know teachers who are gay who have been told by their head teacher they shouldn't come out at school, or share any personal information about themselves. Straight teachers talk about their partners and children and home life, and that is never questioned. So what are we saying to children? That being gay is something to be ashamed of and hidden away?'

Navah is, though, conscious that many teachers don't want to talk about sex, and she says that the charity has to remind them that their workshops have nothing to do with sex education. 'There is a link between sex and sexuality that we need to break,' she says. 'Sexuality is about relationships, about who you love, who you go on to have a life and a family with. The work we do focuses on relationships and about respect for other people who might be different from you because they have a different sort of relationship. That's it – it's that simple. In our workshops we try and encourage the children to celebrate all sorts of differences, and when we talk about homophobia, we draw comparisons between homophobia and transphobia and racism and sexism and ableism. It's important for children to understand that all discrimination based on differences is exactly the same. And the fight is everyone's fight – it shouldn't just be left to people who are LGBT. Men fought for gender equality alongside women;

white people fought racism alongside black people. That is how those battles were won.'

A lot of DRM's supporters question how effective this can be in faith schools, with so many debates about the role of religion in classrooms. 'Sometimes teachers cite religion – the mix of faiths and cultures in a school – as the reason this might not work,' says Navah. 'We know culture and religion feed into some of the discrimination we see, and of course we meet children who, perhaps because of their background or religion, find this issue difficult. But we ask all the students to write their thoughts and questions on Post-it notes so we can answer them without the students being identified. I had one from a girl who said, "Is it okay to disagree with homosexuality if I respect it, and never ever criticise it or anyone who is gay?" I read that one out because that is, to us, absolutely okay. We are not here to challenge religious differences. We are here to encourage respect for differences.

'But most schools don't see faith standing in the way of diversity. The faith schools invite us in *because* they are a faith school, not in spite of the fact. Their messages around equality and acceptance and loving one another are much stronger than any religious interpretations or positions on homosexuality. They believe discrimination of any kind is unacceptable. When religious questions come up, our line is always the same. We ask, "Is there a religion in this world that any of you would sign up to that teaches hate?"

'We don't want to challenge their religion or background or their parents; we just want to challenge them to think about what they are doing, and how they are treating others in their school. We want to spread a message of respect and equality and acceptance. Children understand that their personal religious views don't give them a right to mock other people, or make someone feel less than equal. You can see them nodding when you talk in those terms.

'We also know the work we do shines a light on other forms of bullying and discrimination in schools,' says Navah. 'We are now hearing from head teachers who say their staff feel the workshop has made the school a nicer place to work, and that they, in turn, have been told by parents they would choose their school because we've been in. Not because they are gay or have gay children, but they want to be in a school tackling homophobia because they know that school is likely to be tackling all forms of discrimination.'

Developing diversity in the class

DRM knows the classroom workshop alone is not going to make a lasting difference, and it works with teachers to develop a diversity policy that is embedded into the curriculum so that homophobia is an issue that can be discussed regularly, in the same way that racism or ableism or sexism is discussed. The charity challenges schools to consider the way they think about the adult relationships in school life. Why don't they, for example, ask male students if they have a girlfriend or boyfriend when talking about relationships? And girls the same question? Schools are also invited to examine stereotypes in the school, as it becomes clear to them that a lot of 'gay' bullying is based on gender conformity that schools could easily challenge.

'It's the boy who likes to dance but who hates football, or the girl who hates make-up but likes rugby, who are often in the firing line for gay taunts,' says Navah. 'Just giving all students more diverse options at lunchtime or in sport could help. We'd also like to see schools think about the unconscious bias. Why are boys always asked to do physical tasks – the shifting and carrying – and the girls recruited to help care for a student who is sick or lonely?

'We also need all schools to have a policy in place to tackle homophobia, not just general bullying, and consistent application of it. To start with, teachers need an appropriate and consistent line that they use whenever they hear the taunt "that's so gay".'

Preventing the problem at primary level

Navah is in another school now – this time a primary school in north London. The charity's work with this age and stage is different. It is less challenging, but also, the charity believes, more powerful in encouraging an understanding of diversity at a much younger age – before stereotypical messages have started to stick, and banter has become acceptable.

Today the role model is Leanne, a woman who lives with her same-sex partner and two children in Lewisham in south London. This time the class of 30 is asked to pair up and find out three differences between them and their desk partners. Favourite football teams, food, hair colour and hobbies all feature. Navah talks to them about all the differences they might come across in their family life. Children who have been adopted, children who live with their grandparents, children who are Travellers…are all volunteered.

She talks about how exciting it can be to get to know and understand those differences too. Hands go up volunteering their own stories about their home life. Greg, who spends half his time with his mum and half with his dad, or Rosa whose mum fosters children, four at the moment... Navah asks them if they know anyone who has two mums or two dads, and the children volunteer how this might be, which covers everything from step-parents to the dad who might have a secret girlfriend. So far no mention of same-sex partners.

So then they're asked to guess things about Leanne, and about what makes her different from them. They hazard a guess at her age ('at least 20,' says one); where she lives and what she does ('a nurse,' says another girl, 'she has a kind face'). They reckon she is married with three children and is a teacher. She probably has a dog and likes swimming and chocolate ice cream. 'No,' says someone. 'Vanilla, with chocolate sauce.' There is laughter, competition to see who is right.

Then Leanne explains who is right and who is wrong. She is married, she says, to a woman called Mary, and they have two children. She passes round wedding photos, pictures of her children on their first day of school. She is 42 and stays at home and looks after them while her wife goes to work. But they are right about the vanilla ice cream and the dog. She asks if the students have any questions. They do, and they range from the name of her dog to how she managed to have children with another woman. She answers each one in turn, responding to the last one with, 'We had some help from a hospital.'

'Any surprises?' asks Navah. Hands go up again.

'I really thought you were only 20,' says one. 'I can't believe you're 42.'

'And I'm really surprised you live in Lewisham,' says another. 'Why would you go south of the river?'

Putting kindness on the curriculum

DRM feels that their work is contributing to the current debate about the nature of education, and priorities in the classroom, and how sometimes schools need more than a once-a-week PSHE (personal, social and health education) lesson to teach children how differences – an understanding and celebration of them – can make a class stronger, and how kindness and respect can be talked about as signs of greatness. They reckon, too, that many children have to wait until they are living and working and meeting people who are different from themselves to realise that kindness and respect for those people can add something to their own lives.

'I know too many adults who look back and regret not learning that at school,' says Navah. 'Not learning how much respect and kindness matter, and what a powerful force they can be. We need to open young people's eyes to other people's struggles and show them that their emotional intelligence – and empathy is a mark of that – is as important as anything else they develop at school.

'Why not discuss in class what it means to be happy, and to make others happy? Why not encourage students to think about what difference their kindness could make to the world? Why not ask them how it feels to be accepted for who you are, and to accept others for who they are? Or how great it feels to stand up for each other, and for what is right, rather than to feel pressured to follow the pack in order to be popular, even if it means hurting someone else and doing something wrong? As schools strive to help their students achieve, it would be great to see demonstrable kindness and acceptance and respect as an important part of that success story,' says Navah.

'At Diversity Role Models we find these issues so exciting. To see schools giving children the emotional language and the tools and the support to help them think about these things, and develop these skills, and achieve so much more as they do that is just so satisfying.'

The charity recognises what they offer – via their role models – is such a simple idea, and maybe that's why it's so effective. 'It's all about the human connection,' says Navah. 'When you meet someone and like them and learn about their work and their background and get to know them, suddenly who they love, or the colour of their skin, or whether they have a disability or are rich or poor – none of that matters. Our role models tell teachers and children how wonderful and life-affirming it is to be accepted for who you are, and the difference it can make to everything when a friend stands by you, not seeing difference as a reason to change anything about the friendship.

'Over and over we see classes surprised when they meet people who don't conform to the stereotypical view of a gay or bisexual or transgender person. In that hour when they work with them, have a laugh with them, share stories, something changes. Young people today are pretty awesome. They will step up and do the right thing if you support them to do that.'

Note: The names of the students used in this chapter have been changed.

Resources

Diversity Role Models at www.diversityrolemodels.org.
Stonewall at www.stonewall.org.

HOW CAN DIVERSITY ROLE MODELS HELP YOU?

Diversity Role Models (DRM) is a national charity working to eliminate homophobic and transphobic bullying, and they are now offering workshops and teacher training at schools around the UK. Their mission is to help create a world where all children and young people can live, learn, grow and play safely, regardless of issues relating to gender and sexuality.

The DRM teacher training programme has been designed specifically to support teachers in challenging homophobic bullying and language in their schools. The sessions incorporate many of the key messages that are emphasised in student workshops, offering a positive and simple approach to dealing with the issues associated with tackling homophobia in a school setting.

As well as offering a wealth of teaching resources for use in schools, they can support head teachers who want to establish an embedded diversity programme across the curriculum and a specific policy tackling homophobic bullying. To find out more visit www.diversityrolemodels.org.

IN MY VIEW – CHARLIE CONDOU

'How wonderful, then, to be able to give children in our primary schools the important message that everyone is different... [t]o not only help them recognise bullying is wrong – most children we meet know that – but helping them see that not accepting and respecting people's differences is also wrong, and is part of bullying behaviour.'

CHARLIE CONDOU IS AN ACTOR AND
AMBASSADOR FOR DIVERSITY ROLE MODELS.

Prejudice is learned behaviour, not something anyone is born with. As a parent, and a gay parent (I have two children, aged six and three-and-a-half) the idea of Diversity Role Models (DRM) tackling bullying and discrimination in schools appealed to me. So when I met Suran, I was glad to support the work they're doing.

It often strikes me how much kids learn from us. I was watching my daughter tell her friends they should drink lots of water, and why. She's only six. But I'd had the same discussion with her that morning. It struck me how kids soak things up, and it's so important they are soaking up positive messages.

How wonderful, then, to be able to give children in our primary schools the important message that everyone is different, and that it is okay to be different. To not only help them recognise bullying is wrong – most children we meet know that – but to help them see that not accepting and respecting people's differences is also wrong, and is part of that bullying behaviour.

It is more challenging at senior school level, when teenagers have often formed strong opinions on gender, race and sexuality, and when they crave acceptance and a place in the pack. I asked a group of boys in one of Diversity Role Model's senior school workshops what they'd say if another boy confided he fancied one of them. One boy's immediate reaction was 'whoa, no. I'd smack him...' The others immediately agreed. I asked them then if they'd consider the option of just saying no. Telling the boy who'd confided his feelings that they were flattered, but not attracted to him in the same way.

You know some of the lads had never considered that as an option, and yet then, hearing it from me, a gay man who they were having a chat and a laugh with, they could see it was an option. Not only an option, but a better option.

The students we meet in these workshops are so open to new ideas, new ways of thinking. They absolutely understand what we are saying. Sometimes they get it more than the teachers who have invited us in. Too many adults think bullying is part of growing up, and don't appreciate how hard it is for a child to deal with such cruel, irrational behaviour. I know as an adult when I meet a bully, when I meet that kind of verbal abuse, I still find it hard. At the same time too many adults don't realise how open the bullies are to changing their behaviour if they are given the skills and support to do so. Bullies are, after all, not bullying or excluding or taunting others because they are happy or contented. They need help too.

Children are a force for change, and it can be so exciting to watch. It was brilliant to see those lads rethink their reaction to a fellow student just because he was gay and asked them out – to see them reflect on their first reaction and realise how uncool that would be. We don't tell them what to think. We just introduce ourselves and the issues, and ask them questions and give them the space, the forum, to think things through, and they almost always come round to a more accepting, tolerant way of thinking all by themselves.

IN MY VIEW – DAVID CHARLES MANNERS

'...the bullying followed me through school and impacted the powerful message that there was something wrong with me.'

DAVID CHARLES MANNERS, A ROLE MODEL, IS A SUCCESSFUL AUTHOR, MUSICIAN, PHYSICAL THERAPIST AND YOGA TEACHER. IN 2006 HE CO-FOUNDED SARVASHUBHAMKARA, A CHARITY THAT WORKS WITH OSTRACISED INDIVIDUALS AND COMMUNITIES IN NORTH INDIA.

I had always known that something very fundamental about me was different. From my earliest memories I had no doubts about my emotional and sexual orientation. When I was a kid listening to stories it was always the handsome prince who had my attention. However, my strict religious upbringing and the weight of social stigma meant I didn't come out until I was in my early 20s.

One day in infants school we had to write a story about someone we knew, and I wrote about an older boy called Ian who I thought was great. I drew a picture of him too. The teacher asked me to read it out. I don't think she was being malicious, or knew the problems it would cause, but that same lunchtime the boys in Ian's class rounded on me and punched me to the ground. After that the bullying followed me through school and impacted the powerful message that there was something wrong with me. Before long I was getting my head shoved down the loo, and the game was to catch me unawares and stamp on my feet. One day they broke bones in my feet, which still give me pain to this day. They'd steal my homework from the teacher's locker and rip out pages of my work. No one would sit by me, and I was never invited to parties. Worse, no one – including my parents – did anything to intervene. My father thought it would toughen me up, and the teachers just told me to keep away from the bullies, to ignore them, so I spent all my time in hiding, and the game was to hunt me out. I couldn't understand what I was doing to cause this hate. I was quiet, kind, and I couldn't understand what others could see in me that they didn't like. It fed a deep feeling of self-loathing that I only shook off in adulthood.

I don't feel angry, but what astonishes me is that all these years on, we're still seeing this hateful behaviour tolerated. The social response to racism or anti-semitism is strong and passionate, but somehow it is still socially acceptable to use homophobic language. When I saw a documentary about Diversity Role Models on TV and the work they were doing in school, I immediately contacted them to find out more. Schools can be such a powerful force for good and for positive change when they tackle these issues head on.

I think what saved me that was my experience taught me such empathy for anyone who has been ostracised, and that overpowered any bitterness and led me to set up my own charity for people who have been driven out of their own communities for being different. The children in the workshops get that, and they often want to leave those classrooms and help make a change. When they ask me for my advice I tell them to listen to their heart and be true to themselves. Then they will become role models themselves...

5

The Travelling Players

Helping You Bring History Alive,
and Racism to an End

'We aim to recognise every single child in this school, recognise
that they are all unique and acknowledge that they bring something
unique to the school and to the world where they live.'

LIZ HAYLE, ETHNIC MINORITY ACHIEVEMENT MANAGER, ST AUGUSTINE OF
CANTERBURY CHURCH OF ENGLAND PRIMARY SCHOOL, BELVEDERE, KENT

In a primary school in Cardiff you can hear a pin drop as a Gypsy girl named Crystal is face to face with Hitler, a man determined to eradicate anyone of Roma heritage in the same way he plans to wipe out Jews. While Crystal's family are fighting with the British army, she's helping a young Gypsy girl hide away, terrified she might join the half a million Gypsies killed in concentration camps. In her magic Vardo (the traditional caravan used by Roma Gypsies) Crystal is travelling back in time to different eras, to witness how Gypsies have been treated at different times in history.

This is a tough scene for a primary school play, especially given that in this area of Wales' capital there are a large number of Traveller and Gypsy families, some of their children now weaved into the multi-cultural mix of students sitting cross-legged in the hall today. But from the moment the children meet Crystal, a young girl trying to get away from the modern day school bullies who taunt her, they are transfixed and transported with the Vardo, as effectively as they might have been by the TARDIS on the set of *Dr Who*. They've already

63

been back to the 13th century, when Gypsies lived all over Europe working as blacksmiths and vets and shoemakers, moved through the 16th century, when Henry VIII's Egyptians Act forced Gypsies to leave the realm within 16 days, and are now heading to the 1990s to see what happened when the Criminal Justice and Public Order Act took away the local council's long-held duty to provide Travellers with sites where they could settle.

Crystal's Vardo, despite its gritty grown-up themes, is a gentle, humorous, beautifully written and wonderfully paced piece of theatre that provides schools with a history lesson too often omitted from the school curriculum. And it tells too many school staff what they didn't know they didn't know when they came into the hall. It was written by Suzanna King, a champion of Gypsy and Traveller families, and one of the team at the charity Friends, Families and Travellers. Each summer – in Gypsy and Traveller History Month – it travels the country telling school children the story of Gypsies and Travellers in this country: how they got their name, how they earn their living, how they have been pushed out and how they hope for a brighter, more inclusive future. The play, Suzanna hopes, will contribute to the latter by opening hearts and minds to a culture that is often at best ignored and at worst condemned by too many people – including school students – across the UK. Crystal starts the play by running away from her bullies at school, but by piecing together the history of Gypsies, and with some help from the audience, she regains confidence in her identity and her future. The children are entranced when, on one final journey before home, she whizzes into the future and finds her nephew has ended up as Prime Minister.

To appreciate what kind of difference she is making, climb into the Vardo and whizz across the country to St Augustine of Canterbury Church of England Primary School in Belvedere in Kent, where Mark Alexander-Smale, the head of school, and Mary Huq, the early years foundation leader, are welcoming a grandmother to help with the Reception class history lesson. She is a Romany Gypsy, her grandchildren attend the school, and her visit is the direct legacy of a performance of *Crystal's Vardo* at the school a year earlier. As she walks down the corridors, she passes under colourful banners of flags from around the world, and walls filled with display after display – including one in pride of place in the main corridor which features a glorious multi-coloured Vardo – designed to help the students celebrate different cultures and different ways of life.

'We knew there were a lot of Travellers living in this area, but we had no real idea about how many we had in our school, or how little we knew about them and their life and history,' says Liz Hayle, the ethnic minority achievement manager and school's family liaison officer.

Liz designed the Vardo display and recalls working on it in the run-up to Gypsy and Traveller History Month when Debbie, one of the lunchtime supervisors, came and quietly told her that what she'd done wasn't quite right, and pointed out what should go where. 'We started talking about the history of Gypsies and Travellers in this area, how many of their homes were washed away in the floods of 1953, and Debbie was this mine of information,' says Liz. 'When I asked how she knew so much, she told me she came from a Roma family. She told me so many moving stories then. How many of the stories on TV offended her, how the stereotyping set Gypsy and Traveller families apart and made them the subject of scorn. Even how it made her worry how she would be perceived in school – she'd come to believe she could be too easily accused of stealing because of who she was.'

Helping children be themselves

The very next week, an eight-year-old student at the school called Aisha came and watched Liz working on the Vardo display, and asked why the school was doing it. 'I knew she was from a Gypsy family and so I told her that it was important to share the fantastic communities that we came from. She started telling me about her home, about their 12 horses and how they look after them, and how she'd taught her little sister to ride. She made me promise not to tell her class, though. She said she was worried that if they knew, no one would like her. "How could that be?" I said. "You are Aisha and you are wonderful."'

Instead of trying to persuade Aisha, Liz asked her to help give the actors from *Crystal's Vardo* a tour when they came to the school. 'She knew so much about her family's history, and the local history – things I didn't know,' says Liz. 'She was telling them how the Gypsies and Travellers came to the area, how many lived here. She explained how they'd provided the recycled metal used to build the huge cob horse statue that sits on a local roundabout. I was taken aback by her knowledge and eloquence and pride. Then, a week later, after the play had been and gone, she came and told me she was ready. "Ready for what?" I asked. "Ready to talk about my family," she said.

'I was so moved in that moment. It was as though she had been watching and listening and judging reactions, seeing if it was safe to be open about who she was, safe to tell her friends that her family were from a Gypsy and Traveller community. The next day she came to school in her cart for the first time. Her mum said she'd always refused to travel that way – at least until they were way out of the area – for fear a classmate would see her.'

Raising awareness of a bullied minority

Suzanna King's play needs to keep touring, she believes, because while things have changed at St Augustine's, they clearly haven't changed everywhere. The charity knows that in the UK today Gypsy and Traveller children are among the most bullied minority ethnic group. One report reveals over 90 per cent had been picked on for being Gypsies and eight out of ten (86%) had suffered racial abuse. Nearly two-thirds (63%) had been bullied or physically attacked. As *Crystal's Vardo* was touring the country, the media was discussing the rights and wrongs of a station train announcer warning passengers to watch for pickpockets and Gypsies in the area. There was, thankfully, an outcry – hence the discussion in the media – but there were enough people who thought that the warning was sound, with little thought about the impact it had on the hundreds of children from this minority ethnic group who had to go into school the next day and face the stereotypes set by yet another story in the Press.

Recent reports have revealed how far the economic crisis has had an impact on Gypsies and Travellers; the drop in work that has left many scouring the country in a bid to make a living, or resorting to living on cramped sites, unemployed, and the subject of hatred from some sections of the public. While some committed local authorities have pioneered ways of meeting the needs of Gypsies and Travellers so they can preserve their traditional lifestyle while accessing health and education services, in other areas this group continues to be the focus of social tension. Cuts in public spending have seen millions that had been allocated to building new sites and for Traveller education withdrawn. Despite Gypsies and Travellers being covered by the Race Relations (Amendment) Act 2000, most government processes don't measure or monitor their health. If they did, the report suggests they'd pick up rising levels of depression and anxiety – suicide levels among Travellers are three times higher than for the general population.

Education may not solve all the problems for these men and women and the older members of the families they care for, but it can help change the experience and prospects of their children. Not by changing who they are –

their identity is as deep and indelible as skin colour – but changing how they are accepted into communities and treated in schools.

'Gypsies and Travellers – because of their way of life – have a record of poor school attendance,' says Suzanna. 'Some reports suggest an attendance rate of 75 per cent, well below average, and that thousands of Travellers and Gypsies are not registered at school at all. One survey we saw found as many as 60 per cent saying they felt that their culture was insufficiently valued and defended by schools, and again, nearly seven out of ten (and that's those who've come forward) saying they'd been bullied. We experienced that racism when we were performing at one college on our tour, and it was a rude reminder of how prevalent the problem is, and how much it can hurt. We were a group of adults and found it upsetting, so I can only imagine how that feels if you are a child and on your own. We know – and many teachers back this up – that low attendance is not always because of the way Gypsies and Travellers view education, but because of the way they're treated when they get to schools. Too often children isolate Gypsy and Traveller children, or fire abuse at them, based on what they have been told by friends, family or the media. Too often schools question investing in this community, believing the children will soon be leaving anyway, without realising they often leave school because of the way they have been treated.

'This feeds their parents' and grandparents' belief that they're often better off – in terms of being both happier and healthier – working for the family business and not going to school at all. It is especially a problem at high school. Children might spend one term there, be badly bullied and left isolated and then leave. But that is not always the first choice for parent or child. Many of these children want a high school education, and many simply put up with bullying at school in a bid to get to college. Kavanagh Rose Rattigan, who is from a family of Irish Travellers and plays Crystal in our play, is one of them. She is currently studying drama at university.'

Can you help make a change?

Liz Hayle agrees. She is seeing here, at St Augustine's, Gypsy and Traveller families noticing that their children are not seen as Gypsies and Travellers any more than a child is judged by faith or disability. They are seen as children, peers, classmates. As St Augustine's celebrates differences as well as similarities, they are hearing from more families who want to share their life and their story.

They are, crucially, seeing their children do better than they ever did before in reading, writing and maths, and that translates into a parent body that feels confident about their children being accepted, their culture being respected, and a community that includes them.

'We aim to recognise every single child in this school, recognise that they are all unique and acknowledge that they bring something unique to the school and to the world where they live,' says Liz. 'If a child is isolated and can't share who they are, their culture becomes buried and they not only lose their identity, they lose their feelings of self-worth. Learning more about Aisha and other Travellers like her has been an inspiring way of learning about another culture.'

'I am happy being a mum, and I love our life,' says Abbie, Aisha's mum. 'And I was getting stick from home because I was encouraging Aisha to come in. But I could see she wanted to. All my kids did. They were getting something out of coming here that I never got out of school. I was a Gypsy and I was dyslexic and the teachers and students were horrid to me. I just wanted to be at home looking after my horses. But coming here I can see how much my kids are achieving, and, while I love my life, I want Aisha and her sisters to have choices I might not have had.

'One day Liz asked me to bring one of the horses in for the kids to see and asked me to answer all their questions, and I could see the joy on their faces, and how proud Aisha was of me, and of where she came from, and that felt good,' says Abbie. 'Then, for the first time, the girls wanted to bring mates back. They were playing outside and I heard one of them say, "Hey, your home is nice and your mum is all right".'

The difference a Vardo can make

Liz believes that most of the children in the school, not just the children from Gypsy and Traveller families, were helped by *Crystal's Vardo*. Not only because it gave them an insight into a different part of history, a different culture, but by opening up the whole subject of prejudice, and helping them think about equality and respect.

'We did a workshop with Year 6 children and it emerged how many from ethnic minorities thought they were the only ones who felt prejudice. Some admitted that they thought it was only about the colour of skin. We have been able to discuss what prejudice is, and how it can affect different people. You can see a real shift in the way children are thinking, and their desire now to celebrate all sorts of differences.

'The philosophy in this school is that the staff should learn something new every day...and that makes working here very exciting,' says Liz. 'I think what we've learned from *Crystal's Vardo*, and all that has happened since, is that if you want to make a change – make a difference – look at the people who are the least noticeable, the ones who seem invisible to other students. Support them. When they feel able to say, "This is who I am", it opens up the school in a magical way. So everyone feels they can say, "This is who I am".'

Note: The names of students and parents in this chapter have been changed.

Resources

Friends, Families and Travellers at www.gypsy-traveller.org.

WHAT CAN FRIENDS, FAMILIES AND TRAVELLERS DO FOR YOU?

Friends, Families and Travellers is a registered charity working to end racism and discrimination against Gypsies and Travellers, whatever their ethnicity, culture or background, whether settled or mobile. It was established in 1994, and has become a leading national organisation addressing inequalities. It works with the Public Law Project and provided crucial groundwork for two landmark legal challenges that led to local authorities being required to undertake welfare inquiries before carrying out evictions. In 1999 it was shortlisted for the Human Rights Award. Its honorary president is Baroness Janet Whitaker (see 'In my view' on page 71).

The charity represents all Travellers and aims to support their self-reliance and independence, shared culture and traditions, and the priority they give their children, family and extended family. That includes Romany Gypsies (who have been living in the UK since the 16th century) and their descendants, the Roma Gypsies, Irish Travellers (many of whom came to England in the 1850s during the Irish potato famine), showmen (a cultural minority who have owned and operated funfairs and circuses for generations),

Scottish Travellers (dating back to the 12th century) and non-ethnic or New Age Travellers, who have often taken to life on the road in their own lifetime.

There are so many ways the charity could support your work in the classroom. As well as bringing *Crystal's Vardo* to your school, they have a whole series of resources to share, including reports from Save the Children and The Children's Society, story books and a practical toolkit and books for school settings (suitable whether or not schools are working with Gypsy, Roma and Traveller children), as well as guidance materials to support teachers in promoting the achievement of Gypsy, Roma and Traveller students, and in meeting their statutory duties in terms of the Race Relations (Amendment) Act 2000. Attainment data shows that Gypsy, Roma and Traveller students' performance is worryingly low, and the gaps are not narrowing as they are for other ethnic groups. Their research shows that when Gypsy, Roma and Traveller students are given the right learning environment, they can be just as successful as students in any other group.

For more information, visit www.gypsy-traveller.org and go to the 'Your Family' page and click on the 'Young People and Education' section.

IN MY VIEW – BARONESS JANET WHITAKER

'When you see schools take this issue seriously, and many now do, children of Gypsies and Travellers – instead of being bullied and isolated and suffering discrimination – are included, respected and can themselves be a force for change.'

BARONESS JANET WHITAKER IS HONORARY PRESIDENT, FRIENDS, FAMILIES AND TRAVELLERS.

There are some 300,000 Gypsies and Travellers in the UK, and they receive an unacceptable amount of abuse and discrimination. We need people to speak up for them, in Parliament, in public life and at schools. We know scapegoating is a sociological phenomenon and a regrettable human tendency. It has impacted on minorities in the past, but while it seems to now get stamped on or at least discussed when it comes to other minorities, it seems to be accepted for Gypsies and Travellers. That has to change, and schools can have a huge role in making that happen – by starting a conversation about the rights and wrongs of how we treat this ethnic minority.

Crystal's Vardo is a wonderful way to help schools start that very conversation – by teaching children about the history of Gypsies and Travellers in Britain. To hear children after they have seen the play talking about what they have learned, and how that challenges what they have previously been told, is so interesting and hopeful. When you see schools take this issue seriously, and many now do, children of Gypsies and Travellers – instead of being bullied and isolated and suffering discrimination – are included, respected and can themselves be a force for change. Their families see the opportunities education offers their children, and that bullying and discrimination don't have to be a part of that, and the school body and the wider community benefit from everything those children and families have to offer.

6

The Achievement Coach

Helping You Think Outside the Box

'The fact is, as a head teacher I stand and fall by our most vulnerable student. It is my job, my duty, to do all I can for them.'

CLAIRE PRICE, HEAD TEACHER, CHEPSTOW COMPREHENSIVE, MONMOUTHSHIRE

The reception staff at a secondary school in Chepstow are all of a doodah. They have just had a call from Henry Winkler – aka 'The Fonz' from the US smash hit *Happy Days* – who reports he is lost somewhere between the M4 and this ancient market town in South Wales, and needs directions to the comprehensive school where hundreds of students are waiting to hear him speak.

'Okay Henry, go right, then take the second left, then you'll see the school in front of you.' The receptionist puts down the phone. 'That was The Fonz,' she says to the crowd in reception, barely suppressing a squeal. 'I just spoke to The Fonz.'

The crowd in reception is buzzing now, the head teacher, governors, teachers, all ready to welcome Henry Winkler to their school as part of the My Way! Tour he launched with the children's national newspaper, *First News*, to promote the idea that everybody learns in their own way.

When The Fonz finally arrives and shakes the scores of hands waiting to shake his, he addresses the children – the people he has really come to see. Before the audience can catch their breath he is telling them how much he hated school. How rubbish he was at English, maths, pretty much everything except lunch and going home. 'I was real good at going home,' he says.

There is laughter, the children not quite knowing what to make of this man who many might not remember in the same way as anyone over 40 remembers him – Arthur Herbert Fonzarelli, nicknamed 'The Fonz' or 'Fonzie', and the epitome of cool, the kind of friend everyone wishes was watching their back. But no matter – the children are soon laughing out loud as he tells them how spellings he'd learned perfectly one night would escape from his brain on the way into school the next, and then he questions the 'purpose of the isosceles triangle'.

'I swear,' he continues, 'no one has ever asked me what an isosceles triangle is.'

He tells them how, as a result of his learning challenges, his parents labelled him a 'dumb dog', and his teacher, Miss Adolf, considered him a waste of space.

'She said I was lazy, lacking in potential,' he recalls.

He then, with some pride, carefully gets out a box from the back pocket of his jeans and shows the children an OBE. 'I picked this up from the Queen of England,' he says, marching round the hall to show it off. 'Not bad for a dumb dog, eh? Is that cool or what?'

Children cheer. Teachers shuffle in their seats, smiling slightly nervously at each other, wondering where this is heading…

What Henry Winkler wants to represent at this school in Chepstow, and at every school on his tour, are the hundreds of thousands of children in this country who struggle to learn in the way many schools prescribe they should learn – because they are among the ten per cent of the population who are dyslexic (like him), or because of any number of learning difficulties that can make school so hard and friendships sometimes impossible. His books – the Hank Zipzer series, now being played out on CBBC with Henry in a starring role – are based on his own memories of growing up in New York, but they only scratch the surface of his own real experience. Hank's best mates in the book and on TV – Ashley and Frankie – consistently help him out of scrapes, and stand up for him when the school bully (the infamous Nick McKelty) makes his life hell. In real life, Henry confesses, they were just figments of his imagination, the friends he wished he'd had, like his granddad in the book, the heroic, loving and loveable Papa Pete. Henry's real grandfather was killed in a concentration camp in the Second World War. But the terrifying teacher that is Miss Adolph in the show was a real character from Henry's school days (personifying all that can be inflexible in schools), as was Mr Rock who represents the power of a good teacher to think outside the box and to transform lives. Henry is, not surprisingly, perfect in the part of Rock in the CBBC TV show.

For all his TV and movie success (and he has scores of movies, TV and stage appearances to his credit), Henry says that the proudest moment of his career was seeing the Zipzer books published, and in England he teamed up with Nicky Cox, editor of the children's newspaper *First News*, to make that happen. In 2009 they launched the hugely successful My Way campaign, which has taken their ideas to schools, festivals and even to Downing Street to promote the idea that children sometimes need to learn in their own way – a different way. Then, three years later, in 2012, they teamed up with the charity Achievement for All (AfA), which Nicky describes as the missing piece of their puzzle in getting schools in the UK to rethink their attitude to children who struggle to learn. And, by rethinking, to tackle all the social problems and isolation, bullying and more that are so often part and parcel of having specific learning difficulties such as dyslexia.

'Teachers have a huge task,' says Nicky. 'They have to communicate the same amount of information to the fastest and the slowest in the class. They're under more pressure than ever and do astounding work. We want to stress the fact that the way you learn has nothing to do with how smart you are, and that sometimes a new approach, more in line with an individual child's needs, can make the difference. What we're hoping is to encourage those schools – those teachers who so badly want to support children so they can do better – to ask for help so they can explore a new approach. That's where Achievement for All comes in.'

Calling in the coaches to help your staff

Achievement for All 3As (to give it its full title) also started life back in 2009. A state-funded pilot programme, launched under the then Labour government, it aimed to help children not achieving in schools. It had become clear that parking these students in a 'special needs' slot, and occasionally withdrawing them from lessons for extra help, was, while often ticking appropriate boxes, not always working. Schools had got too used to boasting that '80 per cent of their children got a minimum of five GCSEs' and not explaining what happened to the other 20 per cent of students, or, more importantly, why. The programme's aim was to transform the lives of those 20 per cent by raising educational aspiration, access and achievement. Under the then Secretary of State for Education, Ed Balls, the £31 million pilot study ran for two years in 450 schools (reaching 28,000 students) across ten local authorities to try to answer those questions. In 2011, the national charity Achievement for All was founded, successfully bidding to lead the national rollout of the programme on a part-funded basis supported by the Department for Education.

'In too many cases schools were simply not expecting some of their students to figure in their final year results,' says Sonia Blandford, CEO of the charity. 'Achievement for All (AfA) has shown it can change that – and not only make a difference to that 20 per cent, but raise the bar for every child in terms of their results, and their experience of school – their friendships and feelings of self-worth. It is actually transformational. We have been a bit of a quiet revolution, but now we are ready to get noisier.'

Sonia has reason to sound confident. A former teacher, pro-vice chancellor and dean of education, and now senior research fellow at the University of Oxford and professor of education and social enterprise at the London Centre for Leadership, as well as being author of numerous books and articles on educational leadership and educational needs, she knows a lot about the issues schools face, and has the evidence to show this particular approach works (see page 85). Now in over 2000 schools, the programme is led by both an AfA coach and a nominated member of the existing staff, who becomes the AfA's school champion. Together they identify target groups, key priorities and develop a bespoke action plan that is implemented through regular coaching, training and professional development.

'Schools which might initially consider this as one more pressure on their timetable tell us they can not only see benefits, but see them quickly. They can feel a cultural shift,' says Sonia. 'Some are so pleased with the result they are extending the scheme to all students on the register, not just those who are vulnerable or who have learning needs.

'I think what surprised them but what they value is the programme's inherent flexibility. They benefit from the outside expertise but can tailor the provision to suit their setting and cherry-pick ideas to suit individual children. That gives the school a sense of ownership.'

Seeing the difference

In Chepstow comprehensive, head teacher Claire Price has a huge picture of Henry Winkler on her wall, and plenty of her own stories to tell about the changes she's made since signing up to AfA. Like the one about the boy who came to her school – his third – a year ago after previously being badly bullied because of some of his behaviour challenges.

'We were told James would only last half a term, so the first time I sat down with Tina, his mum, I asked her to tell us about him, what had happened to him, about what she wanted us to do,' says Claire. 'I just listened, heard their story and understood completely that her priority was simply keeping him safe. She said she needed to know what happened after she left him at the gate, to understand what was going wrong. So James came in and we worked with him and it went okay, but he did run into difficulties. We told Tina straightaway what had happened, without interpreting why, and met with her and started to talk about what we could do differently and how we could improve James' self-esteem. She trusted us now, and was open to ideas. I took him to a confidence-building course run by the youth service, promising I'd bring him home if he was struggling. I could sense Tina felt such huge relief that he was being treated so kindly, and then we worked together to think of ways to work on his studies to help build his confidence in the classroom.

'We haven't done anything amazing or clever or sophisticated,' says Claire. 'We have simply been there and listened and worked with his mum. When we have got something wrong, and it's not working, we never blame him or her. It's not their fault. It's *our* approach that has to change. So we sit down and think about what that should be. His mum told me recently she could cry when she thinks back to how she felt a year ago, and where she expected her son to end up. Today James's behaviour is better, his self-esteem is better, he has a good group of friends and his mum has gone from being someone who would be in tears in my office to someone who is an active, positive parent, engaged with school life. I know James will go on to sixth form here and he will be a great guy when he grows up. He feels safe. Tina knows he is safe. Surely that's what every parent and child should feel when they come to a school.

'We had another student, Alan, who couldn't access a lot of lessons and he might, in another time and place, have been excluded by now because of his behaviour,' says Claire. 'But we learned from his family how much he loved computers so we harnessed that talent here. We asked the IT team to enlist him to set up a new computer in reception and to help the IT teacher to create a video about the school for visitors to watch. He came out of class three sessions a week to work on it – we discussed and agreed with him which they would be – and took real pride in his work, in seeing others appreciate his talent. His confidence improved, and so did his behaviour and results in the lessons he did attend.

'If a child has a problem and I am not talking to the parent and carer about it, who am I talking to?' says Claire. 'Parents and carers know and understand these children better than any teacher in this school. The fact is, as a head teacher I stand and fall by our most vulnerable student. It is my job, my duty, to do all I can for them.'

Making parents and carers count

The conversations Claire and her team have with parents – 'structured conversations' AfA calls them – give the school at Chepstow a real insight into the life and needs of a child, and they are repeated with every parent or carer of a child in their target group. Training in them is extensive, and they effectively kick off the whole AfA process in a school and, according to evaluations, are one of the most powerful drivers of improvement.

'We know that if children are already disengaged, this process can be difficult, with some parents not even attending meetings or events when head teachers talk about their plans,' says Sonia. 'So schools have to find new ways to reach them. At one school we spoke to, where too many parents didn't show up to various meetings, the head teacher visited them at home, one by one, over the course of four weeks until he was sure he had everyone on board. He was absolutely determined no one should miss out.

'Behind our success – behind the success of almost every child – is this new kind of conversation that allows the parents to listen to the concerns of the teacher but, more importantly, the teacher to listen to the parent,' explains Sonia. 'That can seem a huge task when you look at a school with 1200-plus students and a target group of some 200 – but we know it has to be the starting point. If a teacher starts making a judgement about a parent or carer and their child – their problems, their home life, their attitudes – without ever having this "structured conversation", the child's individual needs can get lost. The same happens when a parent has a negative experience of a school (one-off or sustained). They make judgements about the teachers and school, and the needs of their child get lost.

'What we have found – without exception – is that with coaching and support, teachers can create a forum for structured conversations and understand the children better – their needs, their aspirations, their experience of school.

Teachers are taught to listen and listen hard. To feed back. To agree (not assert, but agree) a plan of action. To try things to make each child's life better, their learning more effective and, if those things don't work, to try something else.'

This meeting is quite different from the once-a-term/once-a-year parents' evening-style get-together, or those additional meetings that are factored in when there is a problem, insists Sonia.

'Teachers do sometimes think they are doing this already, but studies show unequivocally that nearly 80 per cent of teachers in schools where we work have completely changed the way they engage with parents as a result of the charity's training and support,' says Sonia. 'In fact, head teachers are telling me this coaching has transformed the way teachers at their school engage with every single parent, not just the parents of children who are struggling. What prompts people to make rash judgements about each other – parents of teachers or teachers of parents – is their own lack of resilience. What we are aiming to do is develop the resilience of the child through the resilience of the parents and teachers.'

The AFA coach stays with the school for two years, and will often observe those conversations, and follow what happens in classrooms and at interventions (such as when the child leaves for reading or maths support).

'Then, at the end of the term, we do a deep dive analysis and look at the progress of individual children,' says Sonia. 'Does leaving a class for learning support work? If not, what might work better? What additional activities might help? We soon sensed that many schools had been happily parking kids with a SENCO (special educational needs coordinator) for an hour a week or with a teaching assistant each day, but then they were the only people on the staff who had any understanding of the child, and too often they didn't have a voice. Everyone in the school has to take responsibility for individual children, and understand their individual needs for this to be effective.'

Introducing individual ideas for individual children

As well as rethinking the SENCO-style support children receive, schools are given a whole tool box of 'alternative' ideas to meet individual needs, and encouraged to develop some of their own. AfA coaches work with them to introduce them into the school day.

'We don't have a list of things that work, and a list of things that don't,' says Sonia. 'It really depends on the child, as Claire's experience in Chepstow illustrates. We know a lot of the ideas sound like common sense, but sometimes schools don't have the time or breathing space to have even considered them. With all the pressures they face, they sometimes can't see how they can make the time to do something extra, something different for one individual. So we show them how.

'I heard from a school about a student who was fast becoming a school refuser, his social difficulties knocking his confidence, which in turn affected his focus, which affected his results, which made him want to come to school less,' says Sonia. 'Through the structured conversation they discovered the thing that made him happy was gardening. He looked after a window box in his flat. So the head spoke to the caretaker and got him to dig over a small plot which he then asked the boy to come in and help work on each morning, instead of going into class. Suddenly, he loved coming in. The caretaker started to put words on the plant pots and got him counting seeds and measuring beds. That gave him back his confidence, helped him catch up with his reading and maths. Before long he was choosing to come in earlier to tend the garden before school started, so he could go into class full time. The school never looked back. In another school a couple of children had real communication problems, so we directed the head teacher to an art therapy training course. The teaching assistant who went on it now runs a "draw and talk" club every day, and the number who go to it is growing all the time.'

The benefits of thinking outside the box like this are abundant, and variations on these stories can be heard coming from the growing number of schools registering with AfA. They are, says Sonia, all sensible, doable and successful, and soon shine a light on practices that are not working but that have become part of the furniture in too many schools.

Helping students through the free time challenge

That furniture, as Sonia calls it, is often displayed in a school at the start and end of the day, and during the free periods that come in between which are, too often, the times when schools see most bullying and behaviour problems.

'A common challenge for schools is children who struggle to come in, arriving late, or who are frequently absent, perhaps because they are young carers, or have no friends, or are being bullied,' suggests Sonia, by way of example.

'We see how these children arrive and get put in the late book, get cold looks or even a "late again"-style scolding from the school receptionist or office, and then receive more negative feedback when they finally arrive in class. Is that going to help them learn? Is that going to improve their attendance?

'Our coaches encourage schools to stand back and ask those questions. They may suggest that if a school simply changes that start to the day – by training the receptionists and making sure they have certain children on their radar and can welcome and reassure them whenever they arrive, or by enlisting mentors or TAs not on duty during registration to welcome and help a child into class – you can completely change that child's experience, and others' view of him or her. Where we've seen those changes we've heard staff tell us they've seen knock-on benefits all day, the very same day.

'We always ask the school what they do with the children's free time, and ask them to do an audit of who stays on for after-school clubs, or which families attend school socials. Many schools that had assumed everything was all right quickly realise – via the audit – how few students with SEND (special educational needs and disabilities), or how few students from families who are struggling, were showing up,' says Sonia.

'Often schools see playtimes and lunchtimes and after-school activities as separate from the learning experience. But this free time can – with the proper guidance and support – be so important, a time when children live out what they are learning in class. Many schools see "break" as a place for children to develop social skills, but don't see that if they haven't got many to develop, or worse, have developed anti-social behaviour or are learning from others that popularity comes from treating each other badly, they are not learning anything useful,' says Sonia. 'I meet too many head teachers who think their job is to protect the staff's breaks rather than to use this time to support the children's learning.

'So we ask schools to think about what impact that has – the social side – on those children's feelings of belonging, and on their learning,' says Sonia. 'This isn't about saying "you must sign up to a club" or "you must come to every school social", but about asking those children – those families – what kind of free time support and socials they want and their children need. The parents always have loads of ideas, and then we start to see schools on the programme launch different types of get-togethers at times that suit all families, and launch – at break and during lunchtimes – quiet areas, organised games, crossword, chess and domino clubs, activities that are supervised by adults and which support the social needs of those who are vulnerable, or those who are too often on the end of bullying behaviour.'

The result? 'They tell us over and over they see a new atmosphere in the playground, and new friendship groups forming. Without exception things improve,' says Sonia. 'Those vulnerable children in the school, the ones on the sidelines who are staring out of the window wishing they were at home, can too easily become victims, attracting the children who are looking to exert their power, or gloat about their success or popularity,' says Sonia. 'Give those vulnerable children tools that empower them, new ways to make friends, they are immediately more confident and so less likely to be bullied.'

This programme is an investment for schools – signing up to the programme costs anything from £2000 to £7500 a year (depending on location, status and the size of the school) for the two years they are being trained and supported. Many use their student premium funding – it adds up to about eight student premiums a year at the top end. But Sonia says head teachers like Claire Price are telling the charity that once they thought strategically about how they used their money and how they organised their school and deployed staff, it was always easier than they envisaged. 'And the savings – when it comes to dealing with behaviour problems or attendance issues – are soon clear,' says Sonia. 'We know it takes time and energy to get started, but we are supporting schools who know they have to step back and ask themselves what would happen if they did things differently. Heads and teachers who want every child to do well and be happy. So we have seen schools with the most challenging catchment roll up their sleeves and invest time and energy, and the results are amazing. They are effectively breaking the cycle of failure and unhappiness and tackling behaviour and emotional problems. They are seeing children happier, more engaged, more confident and focused.'

Pass it on: making the coached the coaches

Claire Price says her school in Chepstow has over 30 children with a statement of needs, and the first year she was head teacher no child with a statement achieved five GCSEs including English and maths. 'That is horrendous,' she adds. 'But we are not in that state any more. First year on this programme, over half got those grades, last year 68 per cent, and now we are looking at 80 per cent. But while we wanted to narrow the gap between the achievers and under-achievers, we also wanted to raise the bar for everyone, including the high-achieving students.

'A lot of political school drivers are about the big cohort number, but you risk then taking your eye off individual children,' says Claire. 'We have seen that if you have a good inclusive school model you start to look harder at individuals. I feel we are no longer a school of a thousand children, but a school of a thousand individuals. Every one of them might have different needs. Sometimes children need help learning to read, or learning to behave, or learning to make friends, or understanding how to access information. Sometimes children need help understanding we are all different and need to learn to be kind.

'I think one of the most powerful things we've seen here in Chepstow is how the programme has changed our behaviours as a staff,' says Claire. 'If you don't help a child who is feeling lonely or not making friends or not managing school, students see that and model it. If you condone meanness by ignoring it, students see that and model it. But then when you stand back and question it, consistently, you shift the mood. When teachers care enough about individual children to put something special in place – just for them – the children notice. We do have issues, of course we do, but it's the way we tackle them that has changed. We've trained a group of support staff to coach children in the way we've been coached. We're training sixth-formers to be coaches. So whenever there is an incident of bullying, we have individuals who have been trained to talk to those students about their behaviour and their role in looking after others.

'If you live and walk and talk equality and inclusion – as you move through the corridors and take assemblies and teach lessons – it rubs off,' says Claire. 'It makes you feel good and, when you give kids the chance to try it, they feel good too. You can see it on their faces. You meet students where every conversation has been antagonistic or aggressive or bossy and excluding – and if you coach them and help them to change that, and give them a taste of what it feels like to be nicer and more equitable, they feel better about others and themselves. You just have to show them how.

'The coaching isn't complicated,' says Claire. 'I had a girl come to my office who had been really rude and mean and she came in expecting a rollicking, and a demand for an apology. But I didn't treat her lack of respect with a lack of respect. I gave her time, tried to find out what was going on, coached her to think about why she'd said what she had said, and how that made the other person feel, and asked her what she thought she should do about it…and she went back out and talked to them. I challenge every act of meanness and rudeness the same way. We all get it wrong sometimes, but our behaviour isn't always who we are, and we need to understand that – in ourselves and in others.

'The truth is there is such a clear link between the behaviour and the learning. Sometimes you have to shift the focus off the learning and onto the friendships, off the results and onto the relationships in a school – look at the impact they have on students' confidence and feelings of self-worth. We've seen that when you do that, the learning and the results improve too.'

That includes those children who were doing okay before Sonia's team arrived.

'If a child is doing okay and is happy, sometimes parents don't want you to mess with it, and are not as interested in how the school is helping those who are struggling,' says Sonia. 'They should know that what we're seeing is that if you improve things for those at the bottom, everyone moves forward. In fact, those children in the middle often don't know what their full potential is. Raise the bar and change the mood in the school, and you can see things changing across the board; you can see children – all children – aspiring for better.'

Henry Winkler agrees, and says there is nothing more satisfying than to see what's changed when he returns to schools on his now annual tour. On another stage at another school many miles from Chepstow, he's pulled the OBE out again and is walking round the hall, talking to children, answering their questions and making them feel great.

'I know that not every child who hears me gets it. They may be doing fine and not get it at all. They may even be the bully,' says Henry. 'Maybe I will make them think again, maybe not. But if I can encourage one school to rethink how they approach that problem or student, with the help of Achievement for All, or reach just one boy or girl who felt like I did at their age, that's good enough for me,' he says.

Henry takes off around the hall of another 800 children. 'This from the guy who was told by teachers he couldn't achieve anything,' he says, holding up the OBE, beaming. 'I got this for something I loved doing, and discovered I was actually good at. You have greatness in you too. Every single one of you. I'm hoping this school can now help you figure out what it is. But if they can't, I know you can figure out what it is – because you should know that this world needs every bit of your greatness.'

Note: The names of students and parents in this chapter have been changed.

WHAT CAN ACHIEVEMENT FOR ALL DO FOR YOU?

The national charity Achievement for All 3As (AfA) was founded in 2011 to roll-out the Government's 'Achievement for All' pilot programme.

An evaluation of that pilot had looked not only at exam results, but also on wider outcomes like attendance, behaviour, bullying, positive relationships and parental confidence. It compared 8000 students in their target groups – mostly those with SEND – with general data provided by the Department for Education. There were clear improvements in English and maths in the target group (in English the progress was better in the target group than for those in the same school without SEND), with positive results in all the wider outcomes too. The majority of those working on the pilot, excited by the huge potential of the findings, joined Sonia's team at the new charity.

An evaluation of progress since 2011 (to 2014, during which time the charity increased the number of schools it worked with, from 450 to 2217) indicated consistently better results, and reported 77 per cent of students listening and behaving better, 64 per cent fewer students recorded persistently absent, and 84 per cent of parents feeling better able to support their children.

The scheme is part-funded and supported by the Department of Education and costs schools up to eight student premiums (it can be less according to size, location and status of the school). The website has full details of the current fee structure.

The AfA framework is structured around four interdependent elements that together form the backbone of the school programme. They include 'leadership' (coaching for inclusive leadership), 'teaching and learning' (developing skills for analysing the effectiveness of provision and supporting the introduction of interventions), 'wider outcomes' (developing behaviours to improve attendance, learning and wellbeing) and 'parent and carer engagement' (the crucial structured conversation to build an effective relationship between the teachers and parents and carers).

For more information about the charity and forthcoming events, visit www.afa3as.org.uk.

IN MY VIEW – HENRY WINKLER

'We need, today, to give all children the confidence to stand out and stand up for each other. We need to support teachers as they create an environment where that can happen.'

HENRY WINKLER, OBE, TV AND FILM ACTOR AND AUTHOR, IS CO-FOUNDER OF MY WAY, THE CAMPAIGN RUN BY *FIRST NEWS* CHILDREN'S NEWSPAPER. HENRY IS ALSO AN AMBASSADOR FOR ACHIEVEMENT FOR ALL.

Anyone who has heard me talk on the *My Way* campaign trail knows that I hated school. I was bullied and I was made to feel stupid. I haven't met a child with dyslexia who hasn't been made to feel stupid. I know, though, that it doesn't have to be that way.

We are at a point in time where we have an opportunity to review how we teach. There is a rising tide of support for education that looks harder at individual children and how they learn and how they see the world – and then finds new ways to reach them. That has to include engaging with their parents and guardians in a respectful way so that, instead of hearing what is wrong with their child, or why their child is struggling, they hear about the positive things that are going to happen to change that. They hear that they can be part of that process – that the school needs them to be part of that process, working in partnership with the teacher.

We are at a point in time where we are recognising that some of the things we teach, and some of the ways we teach them, are rather archaic. We are seeing schools wanting to focus on learning for life – teaching children how to be good citizens, how to be good people, how to be kind. Sometimes you do have to teach that and, just as you get kids to practise maths, you have to get kids to practise being kind, in and out of class.

It is as easy to be kind as it is to bully. As easy to include a child in a game as it is to exclude them. There is something that makes children single out others who are different or vulnerable, and we need to find out what makes them do that, what problems they might be covering for, and to encourage them to shine in a different way. To empower them to do good, rather than letting them be powerful and 'popular' by bullying and excluding. We can teach those children that there is a better way. We can teach them that kindness gives something back, something marvellous. That as a giver they get to feel good about themselves, as well as helping someone else feel good too.

We need, today, to give all children the confidence to stand out and stand up for each other. We need to support teachers as they create an environment where that can happen. There is a saying that all that it takes for the triumph of evil is for the good to do nothing. We need to teach children what that means in their everyday lives.

What I am hoping to do with Achievement for All – who you have met in this chapter – is to encourage schools to think outside the box, and to try something a little different which could make a huge change. A change to children's experience of school, to their confidence, happiness, outlook – and to their results and so the opportunities that are open to them in the future.

7

The Gardening Club

See How Their Confidence Grows

'It's about nature and nurture working together, and for our children, being a part of those natural cycles helps them learn they can be a useful part of something wonderful. It offers the best opportunity for social interactions and social inclusion.'

MARTIN BILLETT, TEACHER AT THE RIDGEWAY
COMMUNITY SCHOOL, FARNHAM, SURREY

Sam, an energetic smiling boy, is in his final year of primary, preparing to head off to senior next September. He is one of those jolly boys who is a favourite with the teachers, who listens to everyone carefully, stops to pick up others' dropped pencils or pens, and who'd love more than anything to fit easily with the others in his class. When the bell rings for break he canters after the gangs of boys, hoping for a go in the game or a place in their inner circle. Often, though, Sam ends up on his own. But when that happens, he always has something to do, a purpose at playtime.

Sam is a gardener, and at his primary school in Gloucestershire there is a garden that he tends, and a gardening club he loves, and a whole display around the front door he can be proud of because it was created by him and the other children in his club.

It's here at this school that Jo Greenwood, the school's visiting gardener, has been spending the afternoon in the grounds with some of the students with additional needs who come out of lessons for some one-to-one therapeutic horticulture. But now she's getting ready for the after-school gardening club she runs every Thursday. When the bell goes, and children spill out of the classrooms, some head off to play football, others to the park, others team up and talk play dates. But several – from different year groups – head to the corner of the playground where Jo is lining up pots on a wooden picnic table. As soon as they arrive they're given a task to do.

'Samuel, can you go and water the vegetable patch, please, and Lucy and Moll, you help me lift these seedlings onto the bench and count how many we have while David and Kuna open up the compost,' says Jo. The group gets bigger and busier, and it is immediately apparent that the children are not necessarily here with close friends, but instead are paired or teamed up by Jo in what seems a more arbitrary way.

When everyone has arrived and housekeeping tasks are complete, Jo gathers the children round the table to show them some grasses she's brought along. She has a sheet with names and diagrams of common varieties – ryegrass and cocksfoot and sheep fescue and bent grass – and asks the children to see if they can spot the varieties from the pile she's got in front of her. They gently examine each one, scanning their sheets, asking each other what they've found. Paired up by Jo, they head off into the garden to see if they can spot the one that is 'missing' from the collection. Then it's time to get their hands dirty by potting up some baskets for a new summer display at the front of the school.

Given that there are a dozen children here, vying for the flowers on offer and the compost bag, you might expect noise and mess and confusion. But Jo's oh-so-calm way of handling proceedings seems to have rubbed off on her charges, and boys who ten minutes ago burst out of classrooms roaring like dinosaurs seem calm and focused, one biting his lip as he concentrates on getting the fragile seedlings out of their pots and into their basket. 'Can someone hold this steady for me?' asks one. 'Anyone got a spare geranium?' asks another. Those who finish first are asked to scour the school garden for some nice-shaped stones to put around the pots, a task to keep them busy before the next round of activity.

'We know some children struggle in their social groups, for a whole number of reasons,' says Jo, director at Greenwood Therapeutic Horticulture, a company that offers schools – including local special schools – gardening sessions at their own site, and which brings Jo's workshops into schools like this one.

'But we also know that a few of the children here are shy and just love gardening. And then there are a couple of boys – those super-confident kids who seem to sail through school – who come here to take advantage of the late finish because their parents are working. What is good about this session is that they are all working side by side. There is no competition and no sense that some are great at this and others aren't. I'm always close by as well. It's essential that this is a peaceful place – the "you're annoying" or "you're no good at this" or "I don't want to partner him to plant up pots" has no place here. But you know, when they are given the space and a role and a task to complete, that doesn't happen. I almost fade into the background, and they have a sense of purpose and a sense of achievement in making the garden here beautiful, and by connecting with nature together they start to connect with each other too.

'If there is anyone who is struggling to be part of the group, I can quickly give them a task to bring them back in, to show them they have an important place here. What's lovely is that as the weeks go by, you see them getting to know each other better. You see those who didn't find the group easy to start with growing in confidence and learning to take turns, and to give and receive help.'

Grow plants, grow self-belief

Jo Greenwood was trained by Thrive, the national charity that uses social and therapeutic horticulture (STH) to bring about positive change in the lives of people with disabilities, or those who are isolated, disadvantaged and vulnerable. Gardening is recognised, they say, as an exceptional vehicle to engage students and to promote inclusion in schools, promoting mental, behavioural, creative, imaginative and social wellbeing.

Thrive's professional national training and education programme saw its early applications come from teachers and teaching assistants working with young people with learning disabilities, and one of their first graduates, Martin Billett, says when he first brought horticulture to The Ridgeway Community School, a school for children with severe learning difficulties in Farnham, Surrey, he anticipated it benefiting around half the children in the school. But so powerful has been the effect on the teaching and learning and wellbeing of students, they now offer it to all 100-plus students.

This is not the kind of gardening that flashes up in supermarket ads, the ones with sunny children on sunny days growing huge sunflowers for their teacher. 'This is an all-year round, come rain, snow or sunshine, kind of lesson,' says Martin. 'The students are out there when it's time to weed, and when it's time to water and when it's time to harvest what they've grown.'

Martin soon discovered that gardening is a brilliant practical tool for linking to all areas of the curriculum. As well as helping with counting and measuring, it also helps with practical things like handling tools safely. 'We play a game when a class starts out called "Safe or Unsafe". The students can choose between a red or green mat as I hold things up – a cane, some shears, some seeds etc. – according to how they perceive the risks attached to the various gardening items. The result is children who learn how to carry tools in the right way, and understand how to work in the garden in a safe way. That means they can love the freedom and independence it gives them as they get to work.

'It's also about the discipline of looking after what you've planted, the joy of seeing things start to grow, and the satisfaction of collecting and cooking produce,' says Martin. 'It's about nature and nurture working together, and for our children, being a part of those natural cycles helps them learn they can be a useful part of something wonderful. It offers the best opportunity for social interactions and social inclusion. There is laughter and teamwork and quiet times when everyone just attends to their task. And then there are sometimes beautiful moments where children will open up and invite you into conversations about their life, conversations you wouldn't get in the classroom.'

How your lunchtime club – and small patch of garden – can save a student's day

'There are so many children in this country who for any number of reasons find playtime and lunchtimes a challenge, and who find the loneliness unbearable and the social gatherings difficult, and who are – in a way – crying out for some company and a safe space where they can breathe out and have a chat and enjoy some purposeful activity,' says Cathy Rickhuss, research and consultancy manager at Thrive.

'Gardens are so restorative. They enhance focus, reduce anxiety, and encourage kids to open up and calm down. Where we see schools using gardening as an intervention tool for children who are struggling (with their confidence, behaviour, friendships) there have been some amazing results, in terms of children's behaviour, focus in class and social wellbeing.'

Like many charities promoting the power of the lunchtime or after-school club – that social, semi-structured but subtly supervised playtime that can be a godsend for children who are struggling to fit in – Cathy has seen how gardening can reinforce positive social interactions and help children connect in a way that they can't always do on their own. 'We know that as children grow plants they grow in self-awareness and in self-confidence and self-belief. It's not just about throwing them into the garden and letting them dig. When teachers attend our training days we work with them on different techniques or activities that work with different groups. But when they take that training back to their schools, we hope it will help children build a connection to nature that will stay with them and help them recover from the ups and downs that life throws at them.'

Sam's mother is waiting at the gate, watching him work. 'There is something completely magical about this for him,' she says. 'Sam is the boy who hates football or any group sport really. He's always the one who isn't picked for the team, or who misses the goal and doesn't get many invites to play. Gardening is now just part of the furniture at this school, so whenever Sam comes out of class there is an option for him, a purpose to playtimes and lunchtimes. He waters the plants and weeds the beds – they have a patch they can nurture – and at this club he's found friendship that has made a huge difference to everything else at school.

'He's no longer Sam, the guy on the edge of the playground who doesn't get along with anyone and who is a bit invisible. He's now Sam who loves to garden and, through that, the other boys in the club have learned he's also Sam who has a dog that he's trained and takes to competitions. And he's Sam who loves Xbox and is a big Harry Potter fan. The other day one of the boys from gardening club asked if he could come round afterwards and play Xbox, and I found the two of them sitting in the garden afterwards, chatting away about school and the possibility of producing tomatoes for the canteen. It was a wonderful moment for me. There was a new confidence in the way he was sitting and chatting that was really special. We're looking for a high school now, and the first thing I am going to ask each school is whether there is a gardening club.'

Note: The names of students and parents in this chapter have been changed.

HOW CAN THRIVE HELP YOU?

Thrive's Training & Education Prospectus offers a step-by-step programme of training aimed at providing an identifiable blended learning pathway and professional framework of specialist education and teaching in the field of social and therapeutic horticulture (STH). This is the process of using plants and gardens to improve physical and mental health and communication and thinking skills. It also uses the garden as a safe and secure place to develop someone's ability to make friends and mix socially.

Thrive's Specialist Knowledge Courses offer a programme of training looking at the practice of STH alongside a specific client group, for example, special educational needs. This training offers practitioners and professionals the opportunity to support their continuous professional development.

To gain the most from Thrive's training programme, call the training team on 0118 988 5688 – they can advise you on the opportunities, pathways and courses that best suit your needs.

Alternatively, access the website at www.thrive.org.uk.

IN MY VIEW – DAVID DOMONEY

'This is something that can unite children of all ages and abilities, so it is perfect for students who struggle to fit in.'

DAVID DOMONEY, TV GARDENER AND BROADCASTER, IS AN AMBASSADOR FOR THRIVE.

Gardening can give children an unquestionable feeling of wellbeing. It nourishes their soul and can calm and soothe those who are anxious or isolated. Gardening is about patience and excitement and engagement with something bigger than themselves. The sense of achievement and amazement they experience as they garden is astonishing.

Gardening is also a great equaliser. It's not like sports, where children develop at different times, and develop talents in different ways. This is something that can unite children of all ages and abilities, so it is perfect for students who struggle to fit in. You can get the anxious, the sporty, the cool, the super-intelligent and the super-quiet all planting up strawberries and raspberries. This is the greatest escape. Kids who wouldn't normally be in the same group, working together without any of the peer pressure barriers to separate them. Then the garden can be a place where they get to know each other and themselves in a different way, a non-pressured way. Where they can discover purpose and self-worth and rewards that are way better than scoring the first goal. Together children can see the seasons change, and taste, touch and smell what they grow. With the right leader or teacher, they can learn about the way horticulture touches their everyday lives (from the air they breathe to the jeans they wear), discover fascinating facts about wildlife (like how butterflies taste with their feet and a ladybird is a killing machine, eating 5000 greenfly in its own lifetime!), and see – with the help of a magnifier – amazing creatures close up and in the flesh. The opportunities are endless, and it doesn't take more than a small patch of garden or a window box or planter to make a start. We are seeing a revolution in gardening, and organisations like Thrive and the Royal Horticultural Society are opening up all that it offers to more schools across the UK in new and exciting ways. I hope this chapter has inspired you and your school or family to unlock the riches of horticulture.

8

The Autism Ambassador

Accepting Difference, Not Indifference

'You see someone who is blind or in a wheelchair and there may still be inclusion issues, but children have an immediate understanding of what life might be like for that child... But autism is one of those hidden disabilities, and there is still a lack of understanding from teachers and children in schools...'

GARETH MOREWOOD, DIRECTOR OF CURRICULUM
SUPPORT AT PRIESTNALL SCHOOL, STOCKPORT

A swarm of laughing, energetic kids are chasing Robyn Steward across the playground of a primary school in London as she heads for the exit. Running this way and that, they call her name and, once she's outside the gate, they peer through the chain fence, asking if she'll come back soon.

For Robyn this is the farthest cry from her memory of school more than ten years ago. When she was one of them – one of the class in these corridors of education – children would taunt her on a daily basis. Day after day she'd go into the toilets only to find she couldn't get out afterwards, girls blocking the door so she couldn't escape. She'd hate the smell, hate the space, but be unable to identify the students who were torturing her. She'd see the words 'Robyn is a retard' or 'Robyn is a spastic' written on the bus stop and go and wash them off, only to find they'd been replaced by something similarly cruel the next day.

Robyn Steward has Asperger syndrome, a form of autism spectrum disorder (ASD) that affects how people communicate and relate to others. It's called a spectrum because it affects people in different ways and to different degrees. Those with Asperger's, like Robyn, are often of above-average intelligence but may still have difficulties with understanding and processing language, and may have other challenges such as dyslexia or dyspraxia. Robyn wasn't diagnosed until she was 11, and endured a school life dominated by being misunderstood and bullied. She left with no GCSEs, only to go back into further education to learn about her condition and to launch a career inspiring educators, therapists, parents and other young people with autism. Today, with one book under her belt (*The Independent Woman's Handbook for Super Safe Living on the Autistic Spectrum*) and a busy schedule lecturing at conferences, working on documentaries for the BBC, and visiting schools to talk about her life and to mentor children, she is one of the brightest and boldest ambassadors for autism and, in particular, The National Autistic Society (NAS).

'I know there are times when friends have been scared for me. Once, when a news crew were doing a story about my life and work they worried about me digging awful memories up. But the fact is they never go away,' says Robyn. 'That feeling of being alone, and feeling worthless and misunderstood. You don't have to dig down very deep to recall that feeling. So I tell my family and friends that I'm doing it to try and prevent it happening to anyone else. I've seen inclusion work and work well. I've seen children with autism happy in mainstream, and their classmates really including them in school life. There's a long way to go before we see that in every school, but if one girl or boy in each school I visit is better understood as a result of what I tell them about autism, then I'm helping move things forward.'

This morning in a school assembly Robyn made a difference to many more than one, and now, at Priestnall comprehensive school in Stockport, she's delivering another talk to hundreds more, reassembling cardboard boxes into a mock airport security scanner, designed to demonstrate the kind of difficulty she has when travelling around the world to lecture at or visit schools abroad. She takes off her shoes and puts them through the box, then her bag…explaining to her audience how difficult it is for people like her to follow sequential instructions, and even more so when the pressure is on and the place is crowded.

Robyn asks the children what they find difficult when they travel, and they are drawn into the story and talk about getting lost or missing their plane, and what they have to do when that happens. Then Robyn explains that everyone has difficulties, and how clever they are to find their way round them, and that autism is just a name for a bunch of difficulties, and that these are some of the ways she gets round them when she's travelling around the world giving talks.

Next she draws a huge jar on the board, and starts pencilling in pennies, as if filling up the jar. She tells the students how people with brains like her own find it difficult to deal with a build-up of emotions. These pennies are like our feelings, she says, as she draws – our fears about the day, worries about a friend, excitement about the next class…she's filling the jar fast with all her feelings as she describes a school day until the jar is full to bursting.

'If you're not on the autism spectrum you have a little hosepipe that filters off the pennies – the emotions – so you don't overload too easily,' she says to the classes sitting in front of her. 'But for people like me? If there's no release, the jar gets jam-packed and explodes. You have a meltdown. Young people on the autism spectrum are prone to meltdowns,' she says. 'That's why they need extra support dealing with some of the playground games, or sometimes so badly need someone to talk to and help make sense of what they're feeling. Or they might simply need the opportunity to take a walk and let off steam or perhaps do some artwork to get all those feelings out when the playground gets too much.'

Robyn tells them that once her 'jar' exploded when, after a day of being alternately laughed at or picked on, her one 'friend' told her that her mum had said she wasn't allowed to hang out after school with Robyn anymore. 'I had a meltdown then, and it just caused the other children to laugh at me even more,' she recalls.

Changing the world of school...

It is estimated that there are over 700,000 people like Robyn who live with the developmental disability known as ASD – this is more than one in 100 children – and around 70 per cent are taught in mainstream schools. And it is thought that there are many more who have never been given a diagnosis. But nearly half of the children and young people who have been diagnosed say they have been or are currently being bullied as a result, and the number is even higher among those with Asperger's. Robyn has done the maths, and reckons there could be ten or more children with autism in the average senior school, children who have what is known as a 'triad of impairments', including difficulties in social interaction, communication and social imagination (specifically, flexibility of thought and behaviour).

What this means in real terms is that as children with autism move through their school, they may not understand the unwritten social rules that most people pick up without thinking. This means that they can, inadvertently, appear insensitive or behave in ways that seem inappropriate. Their social and communication difficulties may leave them with a very literal understanding of language, and they may find it difficult to understand facial expressions, tone of voice or sarcasm. Some children may have limited speech; others have good language skills but find it hard to understand the give-and-take nature of conversation. The lack of flexibility in their thought and behaviour can make unfamiliar routines or situations challenging and the hustle and bustle of school life frightening, and this can cause them to become anxious and upset. It can affect people in different ways and to different degrees, so parents and teachers should never assume they understand one child who is autistic based solely on their experience of another.

Effective inclusion of children with autism is considered one of the most challenging issues for schools, but Robyn's visits today and throughout the year represent one of the simplest tools to get that process started. She supports the NAS' campaign to educate children – to educate us all – about what autism is, to get everyone to look harder so they can see and understand this so-called 'invisible' disability, to recognise the challenges and difficulties children have so that they're not defined by them, and to do more to help children get around the difficulties so that they're able not just to fit in, but to thrive in the schools they attend. She hopes that what she says may open a school's eyes to what else they should find out, and what else they could do to create a kinder school than the one she attended.

'When I share the story of my meltdown – how other children jeered or laughed at me and let it confirm their views about my mental state – I know some of the students, especially the older ones, will recognise themselves in that situation. We all make judgements based on ignorance, don't we? We all need to learn not to be judgemental.

'I was taunted with "gay" as an insult when I was at school and went home to ask my mum what that meant,' says Robyn. 'She told me it was simply when two people of the same gender loved each other and wanted to be in a relationship. There was nothing wrong with being gay, so mum said just to ignore the comment. If mum had not told me the facts, but instead told me being gay was weird or wrong or dangerous and I should keep away from anyone who was gay, then that could have impacted on my relationships with gay people – at least until I'd been put right, or got to know someone who was gay and realised that what I'd been told was nonsense. So when children don't understand autism, or are told people with autism have behaviour problems or are mentally retarded or whatever their parents are telling them, it's no wonder they treat children with autism the way they do.

'We know there are still so many wrong assumptions about autism in adult life, made by people who have no idea what it means to be on the spectrum, and who pass on their own wrong assumptions to their children,' adds Robyn. 'I read about a mother who had objected to planning permission for supported living next to her house. Her argument was that if a man on the autism spectrum was living there, he'd break down the fence and get into the garden and rape her daughter. That is as ridiculous as saying you don't want a man with curly hair to move in because it's likely he'll do the same. A similarly unfair objection was to a man on the autism spectrum training to be a doctor, with people saying he'd be too cold and couldn't be empathetic. People on the spectrum can be empathetic, and they can be very analytical and look at problems in a different way, and that could make great doctor material. I've even heard of parents who have been in antenatal groups and become friends and then stayed friends once their babies are born. But the parent whose child was diagnosed with autism as a toddler starts to be left out of the group, like the others want to keep their growing children away from her.

'That's why I'm here. Look at the children I met at school today,' she says. 'They want to understand. They ask the most intelligent questions. Today they were allowed to see beyond the "symptoms" and the "autistic behaviour" and in one lesson got to know me, Robyn. I hope they'll do the same for the next boy or girl they meet who has autism. They won't have to wait until they're working among autistic people or have their own children with this disability to learn the truth. Teachers often say children become more tolerant and inclusive as they grow up, but that's often because they don't get the facts, don't learn the truth until they're older and perhaps get to know someone with autism, or work with someone with autism, or see *Temple Grandin* (the 2010 biopic of the now world famous autistic professor, Temple Grandin) or find something, anything, which gives them an insight into a life like mine.'

'I think peer awareness is essential,' says Gareth Morewood, director of curriculum support at Priestnall School in Stockport. 'Robyn's visit to our school is a special part of that. She is a great role model and frames in a real, calm and reasonable way a school experience that the children wouldn't wish on their worst enemy.

'You see someone who is blind or in a wheelchair and there may still be inclusion issues, but children have an immediate understanding of what life might be like for that child and what they are likely to find difficult. But autism is one of those hidden disabilities, and there is still a lack of understanding from teachers and children in schools, and people in workplaces, about what autism is,' says Gareth. 'Schools may think they have some knowledge, but it might be based on sensationalist stories in the press or shows on TV, or based on a previous student with autism who might have presented a specific set of difficulties quite different from other children with autism now at the school. What we've been doing in this school is making a continuous concerted effort to make sure there is a greater understanding among all the staff, and among all the children.'

Why it all starts with a new attitude

Gareth Morewood has worked with Neil Humphrey, professor of psychology of education at the University of Manchester, to research this issue, most recently in *Mainstreaming Autism: Making it Work* (co-authored with Wendy Symes), and they have illustrated how children in schools reject people whose behaviour sometimes seems unusual. Studies show that when those same children are given an understanding of autism and realise that this is the driving force behind 'odd' behaviour, they stop seeing the behaviour as annoying, but instead as part of a disability that needs to be understood, and they learn how to interact with children in a different way.

'It can be a real problem as children grow up and their behaviours push up against the norms of, say, what adolescents expect from their peers,' says Neil. 'If their peers don't like it, don't understand it, don't have any insight into how the student with autism thinks differently, they can't attribute the behaviours, so they make inappropriate attributions.'

Neil cites studies that show the power of education to change that by providing both an explanation about autism and the associated behaviours, but also a description that highlights the similarities between students with autism and their peers, and which includes suggestions for the class about how they should interact with that student in a positive way.

'These studies are building on what we know, and what is already happening in some schools here – the school in Stockport is a perfect example,' says Neil. 'They do so much work on difference – and autism is just one way of being different – and educate the whole school to see difference as a positive thing. They then have practical measures to allow children to get to know each other better, to get to know the child behind the autistic behaviour. For example, they have a Manga Club run by a couple of the students with autism, and the other students can learn from them – about Manga, about how to create these amazing illustrations. You see students with autism taking a lead role in school life, perhaps by showing round interview candidates, or helping with transition events. It's this kind of work that aims to help other non-autistic students see beyond the behaviours to all their positive attributes including their loyalty, exceptional skills set, and particular hobbies and areas of knowledge – all qualities that, once recognised, can benefit the whole school as well as increasing the child's feelings of self-worth.

'None of it is rocket science – practical things like that lunchtime club are pretty straightforward – but it's the attitudinal shift that leads to those measures that can be the challenge,' says Neil. 'It's getting teachers and children to understand and empathise with someone whose experience of the world is different from theirs. Sometimes when we're working with teachers we try to explain sensory differences, and how a child on the spectrum might find a projector buzz too much of a distraction, and they'll insist that the projector isn't that loud. Then you tell them that to the student with autism it's like having nails scratched down a chalkboard constantly, or a bee buzzing in your ear while you're trying to concentrate – and you can see them suddenly get it. Then they start to open up to what you tell them about the anxiety a student might feel in a busy corridor, and they arrange for that student, and an appointed friend, to switch lessons two minutes before the bell so they don't have to deal with that. It's so simple, but it can transform that child's experience of the lesson that comes next.'

There is often the assumption, Gareth explains, that because a student with autism is academically able, they should be able to manage school with little difficulty. 'But then kids are thrown out into a playground with scores of children, the difficulties in social interaction and communication they experience and their need for predictability can make life so hard, and increase the risk of bullying and social isolation,' he says. 'And that, of course, impacts on their learning when they get back into class.

'It's every school's job to ensure that students with autism are not put in situations where too much subtle understanding is required, and are not left in busy, noisy places where they might not be able to cope,' says Gareth. 'If a child gets to the stage where they are fighting or lashing out or having the kind of meltdown Robyn describes (and feeding others' view of them which might then be hard to break), it signifies the school haven't done a good job in understanding, including and supporting the child,' says Gareth. 'At this point, it's the school who should take responsibility.'

Why schools need to facilitate friendships

Robyn knows that a lot of the problems she had at school were not just because of others' ignorance, but also due to the lack of support she received. 'Yes, it would have been good if the people around me had understood why I had a meltdown, and understood how my brain and emotions work, but it would also have been good if I'd been supported and so avoided that reaction,' she says.

When working in schools as a mentor, Robyn finds young people with autism really need to be able to talk without the other person over-analysing and focusing on how to modify their behaviour. 'If you listen, and explain to them how neurotypical people think – react and behave differently – you can see the relief on their faces,' says Robyn. 'They can see there may be an alternative to how they are reading the situation.

'For example, children and young people on the spectrum may really want that security of the one friend – really want the security of being in a gang at school. It feels so black and white. But they might not understand that person or that group may not want to spend all of their time with them. I ask them what they like to watch on TV, and they might say *The Simpsons* or *Game of Thrones* or *Dr Who*. And I ask them if they have days when they are not in the mood for anything but *The Simpsons*, but that doesn't mean they don't like *Dr Who*. I use TV to talk about how we like different things at different times, and how neurotypical people often have friendships like that.

'Friendship is important to all children, including children with an ASD, and yet sometimes teachers assume children on the spectrum want to be on their own,' says Robyn. 'That might be the case for some, but it shouldn't be assumed,' she insists. 'Teachers need to understand that one of the things that is so difficult for children with autism is hanging out. And there can be hours of hanging out every week at a school. That can feel like a nightmare. When the children are chatting and jostling and joking there is sometimes just too much information to deal with in one go. It's just too busy. So you either try to fit in but perhaps don't know quite how, and then you can be considered annoying or rude; or you move away, and then you're considered someone who wants to be on their own. That's often because children simply need to let off steam or get away from the noise. Suddenly, though they're not a natural part of the gang, and the gang stops including or inviting them to things but doesn't even realise how bullied and excluded their classmate feels when that happens.'

Robyn says she often sees children with autism being grouped with other children with 'behaviour problems' by the teacher – first in lessons and then outside lessons – and suggests those teachers are doing exactly the opposite of inclusion, and actually serving to isolate the student even further. 'The student with autism can then become vulnerable to the influence of other children with issues – the only ones who seem to want to hang out with them,' says Robyn. 'Children with autism often don't have a sense of danger, and can be subject to backhanded bullying where they are naive and are led into trouble. So then you see these kids getting into trouble with others who might have different challenges, but the behaviour – the increasingly bad behaviour – confirms all the misconceptions about autism and, at the same time, isolates them even further. Schools that let this happen are doing the children a great disservice.'

Instead, Robyn suggests what students like her need is adults to help facilitate friendships. 'Not to force a child with autism to modify their behaviour, but to help them see they might be reading the situation wrongly and to explain to the class group – to everyone in the school, including the catering and caretaking staff – the communication difficulties that child has, and so help build bridges before the child becomes isolated or marginalised.'

Robyn says the talks she gives were partly inspired by a programme to promote disability in schools. She was asked to be part of it, but was aware that many of the stories the children heard were big, Paralympic-scale stories about people climbing Everest or becoming famous. 'They can be so inspiring, but it also struck me that it can make young people feel that to be successful and to get the respect they deserve they need to do something newsworthy. That isn't the case, of course. I want children to relate to my difficulties in a school setting, because that is where they are right now, and so where children with a disability need most help being accepted.'

At the end of the session in the school hall, when Robyn has answered what seems like a million questions, she has the children in fits of laughter singing her own song – 'I don't like triangle sandwiches when I am not wearing socks and shoes' – and goes into a supersonic but beautifully clear talk about the sensory issues that children with autism face. How children like her can experience over- or under-sensitivity to sounds, touch, tastes, smells, light or colours, and what happens when they do – stories that have the children hanging on her every word and thinking hard about their own world and how they interact with it.

'That was sick, Miss,' says one girl. 'Wicked!' says another.

'Young people are amazing. They are so ready and willing to learn,' says Robyn. 'They have so many questions and ideas and sometimes someone will put their hand up and tell me they're on the spectrum, or that their brother has autism. I haven't asked them to do that, but I really like it when they do because it's like saying they feel they can be themselves. They know, in that moment, they are understood.'

Resources

Morewood, G. D., Humphrey, N. and Symes, W. (2011) 'Mainstreaming autism: making it work.' *Good Autism Practice Journal*, 2 December, 62–68. Available at www.gdmorewood. com/userfiles/G%20Morewood%20-%20GAP%20Article.pdf, accessed on 26 February 2015.

Morewood, G. D. and Drews, D. (2013) 'Analysing the everyday interactions of autistic students.' *Every Child Update 27*. Imaginative Minds. Available at www.teachingtimes.com.

Stobart, A. (2012) 'Bullying and autism spectrum disorders: A guide for school staff.' Available at www.autism.org/working-with/education/educational-professionals-in-schools/resources-for-teachers/bullying-and-autism.

HOW CAN THE NATIONAL AUTISTIC SOCIETY HELP YOU?

The National Autistic Society (NAS) is the UK's leading charity for people with autism and their families, and provides a wide range of services to help people with autism and Asperger syndrome live their lives with as much independence as possible. They also provide a range of information and publications that can help individuals with autism, their families and staff in schools understand autism, and bring them up to date with latest research. Their publications include guides for parents, children and schools about challenging bullying.

The NAS believes that many of the social problems children with autism face can be avoided by simple measures – like those outlined in this chapter – introduced by schools that fully understand autism. The evidence shows that if children in your school understand autism and learn how to communicate better with their classmate with autism, they will be able to have more meaningful interactions with them. This will help children get to know the child behind the behaviours and benefit from all that the child could bring to a friendship.

The NAS Training, Consultancy and Conferencing Department provides a bespoke specialist service for professionals working with children and young people with autism in a range of educational settings. The aim is to help establish strategies and support programmes that will benefit not only the student with autism, but also the whole school.

For more information about autism and NAS' services, go to their website at www.autism.org.uk.

IN MY VIEW – JANE ASHER

'We could help schools bring out the best in all children, and really tackle the high level of bullying that we know impacts so badly on children with autism.'

JANE ASHER, AUTHOR AND ACTOR, IS PRESIDENT
OF THE NATIONAL AUTISTIC SOCIETY.

When I first got involved with The National Autistic Society (NAS) 30 years ago, we were lucky if people had heard of autism, never mind understood what it was. I went to a tea party at the House of Commons for children's charities, and met with young people representing various different organisations. I noticed one table of children who were sitting quietly, not interacting with anyone else. They seemed different, but I couldn't make out which charity they were representing. I went across to say hello, and their carer told me they were autistic. That carer was the late Dr Lorna Wing, one of the pioneers of autism, one of the founders of NAS. So I had my first lesson from one of the world authorities. I was fascinated by the work of the charity, and by the world of these children – and wanted to learn more. I quickly realised that this condition is very complex and children like the ones I met were – are still – so often misunderstood. So I volunteered to help, hoping that whatever skills I have as a performer could be used to get across some very difficult issues.

Now I understand so much more about autism, and have friends who have ASD. I have come to value their way of interacting with the world, which is simply a different, rather than wrong, way of being. I'm obviously talking about the high-functioning end of the spectrum – I wouldn't for a minute underestimate the intense distress and difficulty that affect those who are severely disabled by their condition. But the traits of the autistic view of the world are, in so many ways, more valid, more honest than the way a lot of non-autistic or neurotypical people behave. I like the way these friends of mine talk straight. Knowing them, working with them, has taught me a lot about the ludicrous way the rest of us behave. Our two-facedness, our rarely saying what we really mean. The biggest lesson I have learned is that I should say what I mean, and not talk in waffling clichés.

It can be difficult to get to know people with autism at first. They can present in ways that don't seem in synch with others, and if you don't have any understanding of autism it can be confusing.

We know that when that happens at school children can be amazingly cruel, homing in on what they think is weird or different. There are all sorts of theories about why people bully, why they run with the pack and are cruel to those they see as underdogs, but we also know that being the best kind of human means rising above those instincts and doing the right thing. Education plays such a crucial part in that. Robyn Steward – who you met in this chapter – believes if children could better understand their peers with autism, what makes them tick, and how much they need friendship and support, we could change what happens in schools. We could help schools bring out the best in all children, and really tackle the high level of bullying that we know impacts so badly on children with autism.

My favourite part of this job is going into schools and seeing the difference the right support can make. Seeing the difference in children's confidence and their parents' happiness when the support and understanding are in place. Seeing the difference it can make to the whole school. I feel lucky as president of The NAS, and, as a parent, to be able to make any difference to any child, and I think parents whose children aren't affected by these issues might be surprised how much they'd get out of supporting youngsters in their own child's class who are struggling because they have autism, or for any other reason. I think parents would be surprised at how much their own children would learn from that new relationship, too.

9

The Dance Class

How Dancing – Wherever They May Be – Gives Children a New Way to Work Together

'This dance that [the students] have created...acts as a metaphor for what they can do in their life. They have shown us here, and demonstrated to themselves, that when given a goal they can work hard, as an individual and as a valued and valuable part of a team, to achieve that goal.'

HELEN LINSELL, ARTISTIC DIRECTOR, DANCE UNITED YORKSHIRE

'Focus!' says the instructor. 'Listen to the beat, and stretch – right, down, up now and across. That is brilliant. Brilliant!' As the teacher at the front of the room directs them, her voice clear above the drum beat, which seems to be faster and louder with each move, a second teacher walks in between the dancers, encouraging them to point their feet harder, to straighten their backs, to lift their chins a fraction.

To the uninformed observer this could be a rehearsal for a musical on a West End stage, *The Lion King* perhaps. There is so much energy in this room the group of young dancers seem to move like one, their curving bodies swaying this way and that in unison, their eyes focused on the wall in front of them, their bodies glowing with perspiration as they twist and turn about to the beat of an African drum. When the music stops, they turn to each other and embrace or high-five before reaching for water and shaking out the tension in their legs.

These young people are not, in real life, dancers at all. Their real life is far removed from the glory of the West End and the backdrop of a Disney tale. This is a community arts centre in Bradford, and what seems like a set of semi-professional dancers is actually a group of 20 young people between the ages of 13 and 19 who are half-way through a kind of dance boot camp and a journey to rediscover their self-belief.

Less than two months ago each of them arrived here, at Dance United Yorkshire (DUY), after being referred by schools, parents, youth services and pupil referral units for a whole range of reasons that had left them isolated and disengaged, at risk of exclusion and/or offending; some were already registered with the million plus NEETs (not in education, employment or training). Whoever sent them was clearly looking for some way, a new way, to help these students out of a hole before it swallowed them up. They've been in the studio full time ever since, five days a week, six hours a day, and are being pushed to their limits.

DUY is an organisation that champions the power of dance to instil focus, creative thinking and purpose in people – including students who have fallen foul of mainstream education. It creates bespoke training programmes working in partnership with organisations across Yorkshire. This one today has been developed by DUY with two of its local partners, Families First and Bradford Youth Offending Team.

When the dance becomes a metaphor for life

'Professional dancers train like this for years,' says DUY's artistic director, Helen Linsell. 'So yes, they are brilliant, but no, this is not about making them into dancers. This dance that they have created and are practising – and which they'll soon be performing in front of an audience on a stage in a professional theatre – acts as a metaphor for what they can do in their life. They have shown us here, and demonstrated to themselves, that when given a goal they can work hard, as an individual and as a valued and valuable part of a team, to achieve that goal.'

The charity recruits professionally trained teachers who believe in excellence, knowing this will translate to the students, who will see their team expect excellence.

'We push them hard, and expect the best because we know when they exceed their own expectations, and surprise themselves and others, they will realise they have potential to do something with their lives and can move forward,' says Helen.

DUY has a well-developed core methodology that drives the work it does with young people. 'It's about providing a framework for this activity – providing discipline, a routine so they know what's expected of them, clear goals, and no nonsense. They have had enough of that,' says Helen.

'There are, of course, difficult groups, and you can see multiple personality clashes when you bring a disparate group together,' says Helen. 'Some of these students have been in awful situations and feel worthless and isolated when they arrive. They may have learning challenges and poor social or communication skills. They may have been bullied. They may be experiencing abuse or neglect at home. It can be a mix of all these and other challenges. We have a strong team who can work with individuals on a one-to-one basis to help support the work in the studio.'

Their journey with DUY starts with a visit to the student's home, where Helen's team outlines the programme and the rules. 'Young people who are isolated, lacking in confidence, and/or who have been badly bullied are shy, anxious, and sometimes have hardly any self-esteem,' says Helen. 'They need to know that they are not going to be bullied or isolated all over again. We always make it clear that no one on our programme is going to be less valuable or valued than the others. We'll choose the groups they'll be with, we'll choose their dance partners, we'll be there with them the whole time – through breaks and lunch as well as classes – and we will challenge every act of bullying or social exclusion.

'That doesn't mean we are fussing them. It just means we have high expectations for their behaviour. From the day they arrive they are a dance company and we treat them as a dance company. These are the rules, this is the goal, and these are our expectations for you. Then – day by day – you see the trust and the teamwork developing. You see students who probably would never have chosen to pair up working together, lifting each other, catching each other, moving together. And when they come off the dance floor you see them holding themselves upright and looking each other in the eye. You see an obvious change.

'It's hard work for them from the very first day to the very last,' says Helen. 'Sometimes we have young people who go through this – work relentlessly – and then get to that performance and still feel they can't go on. Even if they can see we believe in them, and that the company needs their excellence to perform, they are so used to failing, so used to hearing people tell them they won't amount to much, that presenting what they have discovered about themselves to the outside world feels too much. We have to work hard sometimes to get them on that stage because we know when they do it will be magical – and they will feel magical.'

The organisation also knows that if it can get its recruits to that final performance (after which it mentors them for 12 months) most of them will return to mainstream education or move into work. 'When you see their confidence and emotional wellbeing developing, when you see how they learn to work with others, it is no surprise that they can go back into school and have another go,' says Helen.

The staffing levels mean that this is not a cheap project, though. There is a team of dance artists and support workers who spend half their time sourcing funding and planning projects and building partnerships, including partnerships with local colleges and universities, so students on performing arts courses can learn from the programme, and DUY's students can be supported and mentored by them.

Yet even with its amazing results, programmes like this are struggling to find funding, now more than ever. This is despite the fact that the cost of these artistic interventions – and the subsequent return of a student to work or study – is a fraction of the potential saving, in terms of the potential legal, health and benefit costs if they don't.

'You can imagine telling people with tight budgets and a whole list of demands on those budgets, that you need some money to run a contemporary dance programme,' says Helen. 'Even when you demonstrate the evidence that this dance programme transforms people's lives, and supports students back into school or college, you can see they might still be sceptical.

'Then, when they come here and see those kids on the stage for that final performance – students who have been on the fringes, at risk of disappearing into a future where they'll be making demands on social and health services and more – now dancing as if their lives depended on it, with energy, emotion, control, stillness, intention, with others, they turn to you and say, "now I get it". Then they are willing to talk to you and invest in this. It's the same with teachers. They tell us over and over again that they have been blown away to see students of theirs who have, at school, been constantly in trouble or late or absent or unable to sit still or make friends, there on the stage working with others, clearly rehearsed, disciplined and performing at such a high level. They come to us then because they are interested in what dance can do,' says Helen.

'A lot of the work we do is building partnerships with organisations in this area where we work, but we know – with funding – there are so many more young people we could reach.

'I have heard people say you have to meet young people where they are,' says Helen. 'But sometimes those students need to be taken to a different place where they can rediscover what their potential is. Sometimes they need someone to stand right by their side until they realise just how much they could achieve. Dance can do that.'

Dance is, of course, part of physical education (PE) on the national curriculum at Key Stages 1, 2 and 3, but most PE teachers aren't dance specialists, and by their own admission, don't always have the confidence or skill – never mind the slots in the school timetable – to embrace the full scope of what dance can offer. Unlike other sports, dance is not statutory, not inspected by Ofsted, and doesn't contribute to the league tables in any way. Consequently, it's too often squeezed out before a school can discover its real potential, especially when budgets and time are tight.

But not always. Cue companies like nocturn dance (sic) and 2Faced Dance – both working with primary schools in their regions and proving just what dance can do.

The non-verbal communication
that gives children a voice

'Fundamental to all our school projects is an aim to give children a voice to express their creativity,' says John Darvell, from Berkshire-based nocturn dance (sic). 'It helps them learn valuable skills during the process, while trying to steer clear of preconceptions of what "dance" is.' An ex-civil servant who moved out of Westminster to follow his passion for dance when he was 30, John leads this company, combining performance work with school-based workshops, classes and sometimes the less obvious 'dance' projects that he describes as 'a new way of playing with movement' that can work across the curriculum. 'We are not always there to teach "steps",' he says. 'Our goal is to empower children (and teachers) with all the creative, performative and social benefits that come from exploring dance.'

John is known for seeking out unconventional opportunities for contemporary dance, experimenting with interactive work, and for blending performance art with social media. At a special educational needs school in the county, he worked on an innovative cross-art form project with students, staff and a visual artist to explore – through dance and enquiry-based learning – communication and the positive, safe use of social media. To make it relevant to the children's needs, the project was based on the theme of 'How to Survive Planet Earth'.

Later, in an infant school in his area, he supported a Year 2 project on space by going in on a weekly basis, taking the children on a dance journey which explored everything from getting into a space suit to blasting into space to imitating the weightlessness of the outer atmosphere. Now, at a playground at Mortimer St John's Church of England Infant School in Reading, Berkshire, he's launching a term-long programme that will transform pupils into detectives, with the help of teachers and other artists, structured around the theme of 'How can young people learn from others?'.

Each weekly workshop is to last a full school day, and at the launch, John's team have blacked out the school windows, put a huge open crate centre-stage in the playground, and arrive in dark suits in a car at the front gate, dressed as secret agents from the 'Central Intelligence for the Seemingly Unsolvable'.

'The launch is all about firing up the children's imagination and questioning skills,' says John. 'The children have to work out what's happening – what's in the box – and who we are.'

It's not often you get to hear a whole school chant 'what's in the box', but the children are hooked in pretty quickly, buzzing as they wonder what will happen next.

'Each week we'll give them a new challenge and they'll find clues around the school. At the core of each is a problem they have to solve – or something new they have to discover – via non-verbal communication and through movement. So they might have to move balls from a basket one by one to get to the clue at the bottom, but they can only remove each ball when they've successfully communicated a movement to their group: rolling, slithering or wriggling, for example.

'In another scene they have to spell out the answer to a question, using their bodies to create the shape of letters. They might have to form teams to make shapes in line with a clue, or be given objects and have to show others what they could build with them – and replicate that with movement. So if it was a piece of string, the string could be made to look like it can pull them up or pull them down. The project is packed full of challenges like this which encourage the children to express themselves through movement, and to communicate with each other as they do so.

'There is an element of performance in these workshops, but it's more about the process than any finished result,' says John. 'Almost without realising, the children are building on their movement vocabulary and creative skills. Each week they will learn what they as individuals can contribute to the challenge, and what they can achieve by working in pairs and in teams. Every single child will be an important part of it. Week after week we'll go back and reinforce those messages.

'It's great to have longer-term relationships with schools like this one as we can support teachers who might feel daunted about delivering dance,' says John. 'By working with us they can see the difference to the children. So often I hear from teachers afterwards about how dance impacted on behaviour, friendships, attention and attendance,' he adds. 'How our programme reached the quiet child or the disengaged child in a new way. How kids were more confident socially afterwards. Sometimes dance projects like this allow children to see each other in new ways. They allow the children on the fringes not only to discover their place in the class, but also to gain the confidence to take that place and move forward.'

2Faced Dance – an all-male urban dance company in Hereford – is known for its contemporary dance performances that tour the UK, but it also runs a growing series of courses and workshops for youngsters after school, and for students based in pupil referral units. 2Faced Dance has also been into primary schools for a county council-funded project with an ambition to improve attendance and behaviour in settings struggling with both. Called 'Moves to Succeed', it worked so well in the first year that the programme extended for a second.

Impact on attendance and behaviour

'There are so many ways dance reaches children,' says Tamsin Fitzgerald, who founded and now heads up 2Faced Dance. 'So many stories I could tell you. We had one boy, Ben, who wasn't badly behaved all the time, but was really disengaged in lessons and when he got frustrated would just walk out. He was only nine, but he was causing huge problems for the class, was becoming isolated and miserable and was more frequently absent from school.

'There was something about dance that changed that. Ben could express his frustrations – express himself – in the sessions we did, and that made him more self-aware, and more trusting of the other pupils. He was working with others and trusting them for the first time. He's just moved up happily into secondary. He comes to after-school dance with us too.

'This isn't about giving kids a bit of fun at lunchtime,' says Tamsin. 'It isn't like after-school ballet or an alternative to the more traditional PE class.

Of course we want the children to enjoy the dance sessions, and teachers say many become motivated to come to school as a result of spending time with the company – as a result of learning this fusion of contemporary and break and street dance we offer them. We introduced the idea of breakfast breakdance not only to get reluctant kids in, but also to get them focused before the bell. But a lot of kids who are struggling with lessons or with their peer groups are scared, and actually might prefer to hide in the back of a maths class rather than stand up in front of one of our guys with all their peers and try a breakdance move.

'I think like other dance companies we have to face that funding issue head-on. The question of how dance deserves the cut of a shrinking budget is always going to be a challenge,' says Tamsin. 'I think people's reference points for dance are very commercial. They think of programmes like *Strictly* or *You Can Dance* or one of those other dance shows. They don't necessarily see the emotional, health and learning benefits of this.

'And even in schools where they do, if a limited budget means they have to choose between a dance project and a supply teacher, they generally go for the teacher to meet the immediate need they have, rather than dance. We need to change people's perception of learning – help them understand how some children need something extra to help them express themselves or to interact with each other before they can learn effectively,' says Tamsin. 'We see really clever children who've disappeared inside their shell and stopped trying. And we also see those who really struggle to learn and so lack confidence. Dance reaches both of those extremes.'

Tamsin and John would like to see dance used across the curriculum, and in those schools where they've worked they've given staff strategies to make that happen.

'When a pupil is getting hyper or aggressive,' says Tamsin, 'there is a move where children have to do what we call a plank, which is lying on the floor leaning up on their forearms and looking ahead – channelling their energy or aggression into the floor. Getting kids to take a moment and do that stretch can refocus them on the next academic task.'

But it is working together and dancing as a group that is especially powerful. 'Through dance they can learn to focus, to express frustrations without hitting out. They can let go of all that stuff they're holding on to,' says Tamsin. 'They can learn how to interact and communicate with others, without having to say a word; learn how to trust others, sometimes for the first time, as they work as a team. They develop a physical sense of self, and a great self-awareness as a result.

'When I'm working with the professional company on a performance we might share an experience of something and bring those experiences, those feelings, to the dance, improvising and developing thoughts and ideas,' says Tamsin. 'We can apply that technique to our classes in schools, using them to help children think about a lot of stuff they keep locked away. It's too often the case that children are not focusing in classes because they're frustrated, or bullied. This leaves them scared and isolated.

'Creating dances, however, encourages them to express those experiences. Then you can open up those feelings in a positive rather than a negative way. You're creating something amazing out of them. What's more, as part of the company they see that they have an important place in the group, and others see them in a new way too. The dance depends on them being part of it.'

HOW CAN THESE DANCE CHARITIES HELP YOU?

Youth Dance England provides training and development opportunities for both young people and for teachers and practitioners who work with children and young people. For details of national programmes and continuing professional development courses, visit www.yde.org.uk.

Dance United Yorkshire's (DUY) performances are open to the public, and can give you a glimpse of what they achieve. DUY offers a programme of training and artist development, including an introduction to DUY's 'Social Inclusion Practice in Dance', which is suitable for dancers and non-dancers who work with challenging groups or young people with complex needs. The training looks at behaviour management, group processes, boundaries and endings within the context of its award-winning Academy programme. Those who graduate from the first course are sometimes invited to work or volunteer with DUY. Check out DUY's website for more information or contact DUY for advice via www.duy.com.

nocturn dance's (sic) professional pieces combine site-specific work, social media and online video to tell interesting narratives and enable audiences to engage beyond the confines of a stage. They offer tailor-made dance days/weeks or extra-curricular school clubs to suit schools' settings and needs as a one-off or as a series of workshops and ongoing tuition and dance support. For more details, visit www.nocturndance.co.uk.

2Faced Dance is a male urban contemporary dance company founded and directed by Tamsin Fitzgerald and working with schools across Herefordshire where they are based. The dancers – a professional company – also tour the UK and Europe. For more information on their dance courses and work with schools, visit www.2faceddance.co.uk.

IN MY VIEW – LINDA JASPER

'For children and young people who are on the edge of their
class or peer group this can be an amazing thing.'

LINDA JASPER, MBE, DANCER AND TEACHER, IS FOUNDER OF YOUTH DANCE
ENGLAND WHICH SHE LAUNCHED IN 2004 WITH A VIEW TO BRINGING
THE BENEFITS OF DANCE TO MORE CHILDREN AND YOUNG PEOPLE.

Dance offers children and young people a unique way of learning.
It brings together imagination and physical literacy – the skill and
understanding to communicate through bodily movement – in a
way that nothing else does. It allows students to use their body –
this amazing instrument we all have – to move in space and time to
express themselves, and to express ideas that go beyond themselves.
For children and young people who are on the edge of their class or
peer group this can be an amazing thing. If they feel alienated they
can find it a huge relief to express those feelings, especially if they
find that difficult to do with the spoken word or in their written work.
In dance they can relate to others in a non-verbal way and open up an
empathetic interaction. Dance is a collaborative art form, a communal

activity. You have to learn how to trust others – even by sharing a space with them – and to move with them and to build on that trust as the dance develops.

The projects in this chapter touched on some of the powerful ways dance can support students who feel alienated or isolated, and demonstrated the vital role of a trained adult to lead the sessions and to broker the relationships that can flourish through the dance. We hope you will give it a try, and see the difference.

10

The Young Carers Campaign

Introducing the Children You May Hardly Know

'When I started out as a teacher it would never have occurred to me that a child who is tired in class, or frequently absent, or who is oversensitive, or who kicks off in the playground behaves that way because he's been up since 6am caring for a sick parent...the training we've had on this scheme has changed that, for me and every member of staff in the school.'

SARAH JOHNSON, HEAD TEACHER, ALEXANDRA
PARK PRIMARY SCHOOL, STOCKPORT

It's 4pm on a Thursday afternoon in a small town north of Birmingham, and 30 children and teenagers are hanging around the door of the local community hall, some boys kicking a ball around on the grass outside, some teenagers, perched on a bench, looking at mobile phone messages, while younger ones head into the hall and dive into boxes of toys or call dibs on the table football. A group of men and women, turning out boxes of sandwiches and biscuits and preparing trays of drinks, welcome them by name as they arrive.

'How did the test go today, Vina?'

'Is that a new football shirt, Adrian?'

It seems like an average group of youngsters meeting up at a youth club after a day at school.

There is, though, nothing average about these youngsters at all. When they go home after this session – a precious 90 minutes in their school week – there will be jobs to do. One 11-year-old boy called Tom is helping his single mum through her chemotherapy, getting up in the night every time she calls for help, preparing breakfast for her and his younger sister, tidying up, ready for the nurse's visit arranged for the next day while he's at school. A 13-year-old, Maia, will be going home to help her mum and three younger brothers while her dad, a lorry driver, is away at work. One of her brothers, Karim, is seven and blind and physically disabled, needing constant care. 'Sometimes I help get him and my brothers ready for bed – sometimes I make tea and tidy up while mum does it.' One seven-year-old, Lizzie, says she gets strange looks when children see her older brother who has cerebral palsy and can't walk or talk. 'It feels like they don't want to come near us,' she says. A teenager, Lauren, focuses on her phone, chewing gum. Her mum has a mental health condition that has been ongoing for some years, and she spends most of her evenings looking after her younger sister as well as spending hours every day talking to her mum, persuading her to eat and to take her medication. Last night Lauren organised a babysitter so she could go with some friends to a club, but was called home after an hour. 'Look at this text,' she says. '"WHY DID YOU HAVE TO LEAVE LAUREN? IT WAS A BLAST. HOPE YOUR MUM REALISES WHAT YOU MISSED AND F****** APPRECIATES IT. Kx." Like my mum can realise,' Lauren says, turning to look out the window. 'They have no idea.'

Other teenagers have similar stories to tell: about a dad who needs help going up and down the stairs and getting to the bathroom since his stroke, and about a mum who relies on them to do the shopping and school pick-ups since developing agoraphobia.

These extraordinary children are part of the UK's army of young carers and it's thought there could be as many as 700,000 in school today. Not yet 18, these children and teenagers care for parents and siblings and other family members, including grandparents – sometimes for many hours every day. New youngsters join their ranks all the time, children whose parents have been diagnosed with a disease like cancer, whose family has just welcomed a new baby born with a disability, whose parents develop mental health issues or who are struggling with addiction, whose parents or sibling are disabled in an accident…

The life the schools don't see

Carers Trust knows that for these young people schools can either be a haven or a hell, either a place where their caring role is understood and they are supported to enjoy fun and friendships and to focus on their work, or a place that simply adds to the pressure they already feel as they struggle to meet the demands of the morning bell, or the timetable of work, and where they feel isolated or bullied by peers as a result of not quite fitting in like the rest of the students in their class. In their Young Adult Carers at School survey, Carers Trust found that more than four in ten young carers had no one particular adult at school who recognised them as a carer, or who helped them as a result. In fact, most of the two-thirds who had informed staff of their caring role had not seen the point or felt the benefit.

Being a young carer is not, says Carers Trust, something children can announce as they rush into class five minutes after the bell in the same way children blame a car breakdown or late bus or even the arrival of a new baby. Many children are scared by a parent's new diagnosis and the upset they are seeing at home. As many as a third of young carers are supporting family with mental health conditions or addiction issues that they can find hard to explain or talk about. Some families feel guilty about how much their children have to do to help. Some children – when supporting siblings with learning disabilities – are also coping with their brother or sister's refusal to get in the car and go to school each morning, the bullying they face at school, the meltdowns they have when they get home at night, and their parents' resulting stress and exhaustion.

'Bear in mind that some of these children get up and sort out breakfast or their uniform (or both) as well as helping care for their siblings or parents,' says Daniel Phelps, development manager for young carers and young adult carers at Carers Trust. 'And when they arrive they might get told off for being late, or forgetting their PE kit, and then be handed a detention if they haven't delivered homework. At best they avoid all that, but get to class tired and unable to focus. These children need friends more than anyone, but often end up feeling isolated and bullied as a result of what they do at home.'

Given that bullying thrives in an atmosphere of imbalance (see Chapter 2 earlier), it doesn't take much of a stretch to see how young carers become victims. They can be singled out quickly because they have a mum or dad, brother or sister who is obviously ill or disabled. Some children have even experienced the school gate crowd (parents *and* children) making a wide berth round them and their sibling with a disability as they arrive. Their biggest challenge, though, is often the lack of a close-knit group of friends, groups that form naturally as students spend time together in and out of school.

'These children have far more limited opportunities to do that,' says Daniel. 'It might be impossible for them to have friends back, and difficult for them to stay at after-school clubs, or to get to birthday parties and socials. So there are immediately challenges to their social life that their peers don't experience.

'What we do know is that schools can do an enormous amount to prevent that, and a lot of it is so easy. Exposing the scale of the issue is simply not enough. That's why we've introduced our new schools programme.'

How to make school simple instead of stressful

Carers Trust, working with The Children's Society Young Carers in Focus, is aiming to equip school staff so they can identify and support young carers, create an ethos where young carers and their families are respected and valued, and build bridges – strong, visible, proactive, fully functioning bridges – between their home and school and support services like the Carers Club in Birmingham. They launched the programme by locating 15 early implementation sites in 15 different regions, but are inviting all schools around the UK to register for training, and, at the same time, to access termly newsletters, additional tools and resources. Their ambition is huge. One young carer slipping under the radar and not getting the support they need is, they say, one young carer too many.

'Once schools have identified young carers, simple things – like some flexibility about arrival times, being allowed to use the phone at lunchtime, homework support in school (perhaps a lunchtime homework club), peer mentoring – can make the biggest of differences,' says Daniel. 'We want young carers' roles at home, and the support they might need, to be part of the parcel of information that teachers privately and sensitively discuss with their students' parents or guardians so that schools can present the help that's available and give them the flexibility and support they need to get the most out of school.'

Carers Trust wants to help raise awareness among other students and families too. 'We know that when it's made clear that this is a fairly common experience, other families are encouraged to think about the issue too,' says Daniel. 'They might recognise that this could happen to them – to their children – anytime, any day soon, and so think harder about how they can support the young carers in their own child's class, be it by offering lifts so the young carer can go to school socials, or by encouraging friendships so the young carer is not isolated by the extraordinary job they do when they get home.'

'The truth is, when I was training we had just one afternoon on special needs, inclusion and diversity issues,' says Sarah Johnson, head teacher at Alexandra Park Primary School, Stockport, which is now working with Carers Trust on this programme. 'When I started out as a teacher it would never have occurred to me that a child who is tired in class, or frequently absent, or who is oversensitive, or who kicks off in the playground behaves that way because he's been up since 6am caring for a sick parent. But the campaign is raising awareness of young carers, and the training we've had on this scheme has changed that, for me and every member of staff in the school.

'I think for too long in too many schools, parents and their children have simply felt embarrassed to share what was going on at home, and to ask for help,' says Sarah. 'That's especially the case when there are mental health issues. They don't want a label, and they don't want to be blamed for how this is creating problems for their child at school. Our job is never to be judgemental, but instead to help create a setting where a child can feel safe and happy and valued so they can learn. We need to shift things so families see that any barriers to learning are our responsibility to overcome, and not their fault.

'We've now tried to create a school where our understanding of young carers, and some of the health problems their families face, is evident in the way we approach and talk to families when they join the school or later, when we notice their child is often late or absent or not doing so well in the class. We're also raising the profile of young carers in displays, in brochures and in the way we signpost outside support groups.'

The difference you can make by helping friendships flourish

At St Christopher's Academy, a primary school in Dunstable, Bedfordshire, the school's family worker, Lorraine Harris, has signed up for the programme and is now back in school, playing with three girls from Year 4 in the school's new nurture room, a colourful, cosy, decorated room full of toys and crayons, with cushions scattered on the carpet. This is what Lorraine calls a bridge-building session, where she is giving one nine-year-old, Eleanor, the space and time to get to know her peers, Amber and Alex.

'Eleanor's world is different from theirs,' says Lorraine. 'From when she first came to school she was facing questions about what was wrong with her brother, Simon (who has a severe disability and is in a wheelchair), and why he speaks and looks and sometimes shouts out the way he does. Eleanor's not embarrassed by him. She's grown up knowing it's who her brother Simon is and what he's like, and she does so much to help her mum at home. She loves her family to bits. She did, though, start to worry about what others thought. Why they looked at him so hard, and asked so many questions. We've identified three other young carers as well – two with parents who have disabilities and a child whose brother has autism and goes to a school for children with special educational needs. We knew David's brother had autism, but it wasn't until we had training that we understood how that might impact on his life and his friendship groups. Having a sibling who has difficulties can make children cross and frustrated, but it can also make them kind and protective, and so rather vulnerable too.'

Lorraine knows that some families may wonder why young carers are expected to do so much, without understanding that it's not about a list of jobs they have to do when they get home, but more about being part of a family where someone is ill – and that affects every aspect of their life: the routine, the time their parents can spend with them, the opportunities they have to miss. She says, 'Eleanor's mum is fantastic, and tries to give her as much one-to-one time as possible – taking her swimming and things like that. But she has to do so much for Simon that of course it impacts on Eleanor's life.'

Lorraine knows that this has, in turn, had an impact on Eleanor's life at school. She is nurturing, shy and kind but, until recently, completely lacking in confidence. She sees other friendships growing, fed by the play dates and Brownies and mums who might hang out together at the park after school – the very stuff that is outside Eleanor's day-to-day experience.

'We noticed she was on the sidelines, rather than being part of any friendship group, so now we bring her in here to play with other girls; not to talk about her caring role, but to allow them to get to know each other, to cut through the barriers that have presented themselves. And it's worked so beautifully. As they work on art, or role-play, or just hang out here, they click. We see evidence of the benefits in the playground – where they now seek each other out – and in the classroom, where Eleanor is so much happier, so much more relaxed, and so much more focused.'

As well as the nurture sessions, Lorraine has created a worry box where children can write letters about anything that is bothering them, and she answers every one. Like Sarah in Stockport, she's also made sure the school promotes the role of carers through posters, leaflets and more: grants for carers, support for parents of children with special needs, a list of Young Carers Club activities all feature alongside posters for a whole range of different school events and services.

'We hope that by doing this we'll encourage parents to open up and relax about their children's caring role, and access the help they need,' says Lorraine.

'It's about making sure any young carer in this school gets the respect they deserve, and that means the opportunity to make friends, and to progress like their peers.'

Signpost for Carers – one of the Carers Trust's Network Partners working with schools, families and outside agencies to deliver the programme – believes the campaign has repositioned schools in this arena.

'Schools used to be the last ones to refer families to organisations like ours, but since this scheme launched they are often the first,' says Katy Frankland from Signpost. 'We do still meet schools who say they have no young carers, and that it's not an issue for their students and, of course, we know it must be. Every school is bound to have young carers, if only for short bursts of time while family members are ill. When you start to explain to those teachers what a young carer is, and how they might present – late, tired, oversensitive, lonely, disruptive, poorly focused – you see this sudden recognition in teachers' faces, like the penny has dropped. Those conversations have led us to provide all sorts of support services in schools, as well as support outside. In one area eight secondary schools now have one of our young carers' mentors in at lunchtime once a week – they have an open door policy so students can come in and talk to the mentor, and we can liaise with the school, and their parents, on their behalf.'

'Too many young carers feel they are on their own – the only ones to live the life they do,' says Daniel Phelps. 'We believe that by working with schools we can change that. The teachers who've signed up to this programme are amazing. Even with all the pressures they face, they've made room in their timetable so young carers' needs can be understood and addressed. They've helped make sure young carers and their families get the support they need – social, educational, financial, emotional support – so they know they are not alone. They are, quite literally, changing young carers' lives and their prospects as a result.'

Note: The names of parents and children in this chapter have been changed.

Resources

Carers Trust at www.carers.org

Howard, D. (2010) 'Cameron warns on child carer cuts.' *BBC News, Education & Family*, 16 November. Available at www.bbc.co.uk/news/education-11757907.

WHAT CAN CARERS TRUST DO FOR YOU?

Carers Trust is a charity that works to improve support, services and recognition for anyone living with the challenges of caring, unpaid for a family member or friend who is ill, disabled or has mental health or addiction problems. It was formed by the merger of The Princess Royal Trust for Carers and Crossroads Care in 2012. Carers Trust is now working with schools across the UK and Isle of Man. The charity knows there are so many things teachers can do to help these young people to make their life at school less stressful and more productive and, crucially, to help them build a positive peer group and so prevent bullying. Young carers can feel angry and nervous around others, on the outside of friendship groups, or be a champion for the underdog – all behaviour that can be seen as weak and make them vulnerable to bullying. Sometimes young carers need extra time, space and support to build friendships – perhaps via a mentoring scheme or play therapy – and help (perhaps from peers or other parents) so they can attend activities outside school hours.

To get you started, you can access the Carers Trust schools programme and benefit from:

- a step-by-step guide for school leaders, teachers and non-teaching staff, containing practical tools, templates and exemplars

- regional networks bringing together schools, young carer services and health and social care professionals for peer-to-peer learning and training

- the Young Carers in Schools award, enabling schools to gain recognition from several leading charities for effective practice.

If you would like to find out more about Carers Trust, visit their education section on their website at http://professionals.carers.org.

IN MY VIEW – MICHAEL SHEEN

'Young carers can be completely misunderstood by the children around them – and sometimes their teachers too – who have no connection or understanding of their life at home.'

MICHAEL SHEEN, OBE, TV AND FILM ACTOR, IS AN
AMBASSADOR FOR CARERS TRUST.

I am often asked about the biographical roles I have played – David Frost, Tony Blair, Kenneth Williams and Brian Clough. When I made those films, I really enjoyed having a real life to explore. When you play roles like that you have to search for what connects you to those people...and it is a wonderful process.

As adults we are constantly making connections with those around us, and we learn from them and are enriched by their experiences – and by sharing our own. It often strikes me that children don't get the same opportunity.

Young carers can be completely misunderstood by the children around them – and sometimes their teachers too – who have no connection or understanding of their life at home. Sometimes kids can be really cruel and actually make fun of the caring role their classmate has. That verbal abuse can be truly horrible, worse – children tell us – than any physical assault. More often young carers become targets because of the way their caring role makes them different. They may be tired and frustrated, or sensitive and kind. They may not be able to socialise after school like their peers so find it hard to make friends, or they may often be late to school or struggle to keep up with homework. Any or all of those things can make them seem weak and vulnerable, and we know bullies go for those who may appear weak and vulnerable.

We also know children's experience of life and the people in their life shape their belief in themselves and others as they grow into adults. If children's experiences as young carers are valued and supported, they grow up feeling valued and supported and that, in turn, enables them to believe in themselves and their potential.

I saw first-hand the great work that Carers Trust undertakes in our communities when I spent time with some young carers in my home town of Port Talbot in Wales a few years ago. The concept of young carers was new to me. The idea that children, some under the age of eight, are caring for family members on a daily basis, was mind-blowing. As a father to a daughter aged 11 at that time, I was truly astounded at how children of her age and under could take on such a stressful and demanding role in the family, some with little or no support. The pressure they must be under is immense.

Carers Trust not only gives young carers the space and the opportunity to talk about their lives with people who understand, and who can support them and their family; they work with teachers and other professionals to help them recognise the signs of a hidden caring role and to know how to offer the right support.

It would be wonderful if schools could work towards an environment where disabilities and issues around caring are taught and understood. Just by adopting a few simple policies – as outlined in this chapter – their students will grow up with a better chance of becoming responsible, creative and valued members of their class and communities. It could make a real difference to how young carers are treated and they would, then, without doubt, be less vulnerable to the bullying that so many suffer. In fact, young carers could actually enrich the lives of all students in the school who might learn something about themselves by connecting to these extraordinary young people in a new way.

11

The Student Support Team
Helping a Whole School Learn More

'It's too easy to tell girls they need to toughen up if someone upsets them. But our experience is that girls become stronger and more resilient when they are given the time and space to talk things through, when they are given lessons that help them find out more about themselves, and what kind of person they want to be.'

HELEN GORDON, TEACHER AND ASSISTANT HEAD, FORT
PITT GRAMMAR SCHOOL, CHATHAM, KENT

The phones ring with alarming regularity in this small room at Fort Pitt Grammar School, a girls' school in Chatham, Kent.

'Hello, Student Support. Oh, hello – how are you? Good. Yes, she seems a lot better today. Okay, let me check in with her next teacher and let him know. Ring back later if you're worried…'

'Good morning, Student Support. Hello, how are you? That was nice of you to let us know. Let me tell you where we're up to with that. There were four girls involved…'

'Hello, Student Support… Oh, I'm sorry to hear that…'

Some calls (and more often emails) are from teachers, to report a problem they've picked up or overheard in a class, or to alert the team that a student has not turned up despite being in every other lesson that day (electronic registers are updated and accessible to all the staff). Some are from outside agencies to make appointments – CAMHS (Child and Adolescent Mental Health Services) are here to meet a student today and they have an ambassador from the charity Beat (beating eating disorders) booked in to give a talk in a PSHE lesson. But most often the call is from a parent, worried about their daughter and/or wanting the team's advice. In between the phone calls, the five women who work here are in and out, to meet a parent, to talk to a teacher, to walk to the exam room with a class and check they're feeling okay, or to seek out the aforementioned missing student in the grounds or toilets.

'It's probably about a spat with a friend, or a problem at home,' they explain. 'We'll give her time to talk, and then take her back into class when she's ready.'

This is Fort Pitt's rather unique Student Support system, which acts as a communication hub for parents, students, teachers and outside experts, and which – it becomes clear – represents the very big heart at the centre of the school, something which is so effectively permeating the walls you can feel its beat even as you enter the front door, and long before you have worked out what it is that makes this school different. At its core is a belief that the students – and there are around 850 of them – need to feel safe and happy if they are going to learn. That it is the school's job – duty, they call it – to make sure that every girl is visible and supported, no matter what problems she brings in from home, or what challenges she faces in class.

'We simply recognise that if girls are worried about friendships, or a relative who is sick, or a pet that's died, or the fact their parents are struggling or at war over something, then that impacts on how they feel, and how they feel impacts on their confidence, their focus, on what happens in class,' says Helen Gordon, a teacher and assistant head at the school. 'How can anyone learn effectively if they're sitting worrying about something that's gone on at lunchtime, or that is going on at home?'

Helen, who was a police family liaison officer in her former life, says their catchment area is a challenging one, their IDACI score (Income Deprivation Affecting Children Index) is one of the lowest of any grammar school in the country, and girls who come here are from a mix of cultures and backgrounds.

'It's too easy and it's not fair to blame parents for stuff going on at home. To shake your head and say "well that's why she isn't in, or that is why she isn't doing well". It's too easy to tell girls they need to toughen up if someone upsets them. But our experience is that girls become stronger and more resilient when they are given the time and space to talk things through, when they are given lessons that help them find out more about themselves, and what kind of person they want to be. Then they are able to tackle problems more effectively the next time they meet them.'

Making PSHE the cornerstone of the curriculum

The school brought this philosophy to life ten years ago – and Helen Gordon is clearly a driving force behind the change – by rethinking the school's structure, reprioritising how they spent their budget (pastoral care at the top of the agenda), and repositioning PSHE, which is now, says Helen, the cornerstone of the curriculum rather than a class that is picked up by any teacher who happens to be free.

As a result, all the form classes here – the meeting place for students at the start of the morning and afternoon sessions – are organised to include girls of all ages from across the school, not only removing the barriers between years and the typical nervousness younger girls feel when they join a senior school, but creating 'big sister' relationships in form classes.

'We also brought in the NSPCC to train the older girls to be peer mentors – we now have a new quota trained each year – so they can offer a skilled listening ear, and intervene to sort out friendship problems,' says Helen.

The school also relaunched its PSHE programme, appointing a dedicated member of staff – Mandy Lewis – to lead the subject area, and positioning it in the timetable so it worked harder to open up issues relevant to girls going through the school.

'It's about giving students skills so they will be better prepared for the future, and encouraging them to think about what kind of person they want to be,' says Mandy.

Today they are welcoming the aforementioned ambassador from Beat, who will be talking about her experience of an eating disorder and helping the girls recognise when they are getting anxious, and what they do in response to that, and what actions to take if they are facing problems.

'We know that this problem can too easily be hidden away, leaving girls isolated and scared,' says Mandy. 'We've also got a module on friendship and honesty, on smoking and health, on bullying and cyberbullying. In Year 10 we have what's called the "Real Game", when we do role-playing and pretend we are going to a job interview or a cocktail party or a work event, and practise social skills like introductions, so they feel confident walking into a room full of strangers.

'I'm very big on manners,' says Mandy. 'I do think we should teach them, and that, for me, includes teaching girls how to be kind. I don't believe many realise how nasty their behaviour can be, or the hurt it causes. It's too easy to assume that girls should learn certain things at home, but then problems or apparent shortcomings are too easily dismissed, or blamed on what's going on there. I've heard teachers at other schools say that "we hope he or she grows out of that…" But surely it's our responsibility to teach children what's right – we're not doing them any favours otherwise – and to give them an arena to practise those skills and to live those lessons so they can feel the benefit of doing the right thing. We use our lessons in PSHE to give them complete permission to help each other, and then we make it really clear how disappointed everyone will be if they don't take this out of the class and into the playground or canteen – into their lives.'

'And we see the evidence of that here,' says Karen Camp, who manages the Student Support team. 'Many of the problems we pick up in this office are as a result of students calling in and telling us that they're worried about a classmate or that they've seen someone upset. They might not even know the girl, but they do know it's their duty to look out for her.'

Providing a place to talk, any time of day

Student Support – perhaps Fort Pitt's biggest investment of all – now includes five staff. During the gradual restructuring they were recruited to replace heads of year and come from a mix of backgrounds. They never teach and are always available, acting as a bridge between parents and teachers, teachers and students, and even students and their own parents. Clearly passionate about their role in school life and the difference it can make, each Student Support worker – Anna Harkness, Jean Swan, Debbie Williams, Mary-Anne Brown – officially looks after one of the four houses, while Karen Camp oversees operations.

But all calls and emails go to every member of the team, and they are constantly calling on each other's views or expertise as they work to help students in their care, while supporting each other when the problems get tough. Boxes of tissues on desks signal the amount of tears spilt here, and not just by the students. The team is available before school starts – they arrive to join a breakfast club for girls who want to come in early, and leave at the end of the extended learning zone (for girls who need a place to do homework with support on hand). And they are never called on to take lessons or cover for absences. They are, in fact, currently trying to bat away a request from teachers to oversee detentions, insisting that the 'non-disciplined, non-judgemental' mood of Student Support is sacrosanct.

Fort Pitt's head teacher, Carol Winn, believes that together these initiatives are building a kinder sort of school that recognises 'life isn't perfect, and school isn't always perfect', not only creating an atmosphere where girls can learn the academic subjects so they can reach their full potential, but also creating a living, breathing example that teaches children how to be kind to each other and how, by seeking out advice and giving and accepting help, they can learn to cope with problems they might meet in the future.

'We're known to be a caring school because of what we have achieved here, in terms of academic success and wider outcomes,' says Carol. 'We get applications because of that, Ofsted recognition for that, and other schools coming to visit because they've heard about what we do and want to see how it works.'

Closing the gap between home and school

'Sometimes parents joke that we should be renamed Parent Support,' says Karen Camp, who previously worked in social services, mainly with adults with learning difficulties and mental health issues before arriving at this office at Fort Pitt. 'Some days we spend as much time talking to parents as we do to students. Some parents ring every day, and that's okay. Sometimes we visit them at home. Sometimes parents come in here – one mum has been joining us for lunch because she's worried her daughter is not eating, and wants to be around to check on her. Even if they don't want to give us a lot of detail about what's happening at home, they are reassured that if we know something is going on, we'll have their daughter on our radar.

'We all absolutely understand that this is not a place to make judgements,' says Karen. 'We know how tough life can be. We know that one size – one action – doesn't fit all. We may have seen the problem before, but each family's experience is different. You only get that when you really listen to where a parent is coming from and work with them – give and take advice. If they have faith in the school, their daughter will pick up on that. That's why our attendance is so good.'

This isn't, though, a fluffy cotton wool sort of place, and there is no evidence that students are wrapped up in the stuff. It is more of a stronghold, a space in this busy senior school that offers refuge and recognises that life outside is tough for the girls on its register, and that it's the school's job to ensure that anything that gets in the way of the students' learning is understood and the appropriate support is provided. It even has its own castle-like back entrance, stairs spiralling up from the dining hall, so girls can sneak in for a sit-down and a chat without it being a big deal, without having to loiter self-consciously round the door of the office in front of peers.

There can be a new set of challenges each day…but today Student Support staff are talking to a family whose daughter has a caring role looking after a young sibling until her mum arrives home from a night shift at the hospital.

'Because we understand the situation – and have subtly communicated it to the staff – there is no fuss when she arrives late,' says Karen. 'Sometimes parents are embarrassed their daughters are carers – it's often been hidden away all through junior school. But there are thousands of children in this role (see Chapter 10, earlier), and simply knowing there is an issue is enough. We have two staff briefings per week, so every one of the 70-plus staff here is aware of individual needs. We tell the teachers, and they know not to give out after-school detentions, or late slips. They don't even have to know why. They trust us.'

Another call comes in from a parent whose daughter has been upset because of a run-in with a friend.

'She came to Student Support earlier in the week to report a problem she'd noticed her friend was having, and is now in a state about "grassing her up",' says Karen. 'We told her then – and tell her mum now – that she was the best kind of friend doing that. But it's good the mum called us. We can make sure we're all giving the daughter the same message, and keep an eye on that friendship while things settle down.'

The problems are not always easy to sort out, though, and the team can recount endless more complicated cases that they've had to work harder to resolve – the student who felt she couldn't tell her parents she was pregnant (in the end, they invited the parents in and helped the girl break the news), the student at risk of self-harming who they had to rescue from a locked toilet, the students who for one reason or another find going into class too stressful. Student Support has a room connected to the office where the girls can work when that happens (much better, they say, than being recorded as absent) until the team can ease them back into their class and social group.

'Our stats are probably skewed – indicating that we have more young carers, or more problems with eating disorders or self-harm or whatever – but that's because the issues are not hidden away by students or pushed under the carpet by staff,' says Karen. 'Somehow us being here has created a forum – a private, confidential, supportive one – for problems to be aired before they get out of hand.

'We had a girl arrive in Year 7 and within weeks the teachers were talking about her, and bringing some issues to our attention. We thought she was probably autistic – her behaviour, it transpires, hadn't been understood in primary school. She had spent a lot of time there standing outside class because of it. We talked to her parents, sought outside advice and supported her through the diagnosis. More importantly – with the consent of the girl in question – once we had a clear picture of what was going on we spent a lot of time with her class, explaining what autism is, and the behaviours they could expect, how best to communicate with and include her and what she might find difficult, as well as some of the special skills she had. You know, that class were quite brilliant with her, and she had a strong friendship group all the way through school. We bought her this book – Robyn Steward's *The Independent Woman's Handbook for Super Safe Living on the Autistic Spectrum*, when she left.' (See Chapter 8 for more on Robyn Steward.)

Why attendance is excellent, and progress so positive

'It's hard to demonstrate – to prove – the return on this investment,' says Helen Gordon. 'The very real difference this all makes. We feel we're working as a team and more effectively balancing the priority we give pastoral support and academic learning. Teachers tip off Student Support if they have a worry about a student, or ask Mandy to cover something particular in PSHE. We have a staff briefing twice each week, and Student Support can bring concerns to the table. Sometimes teachers don't need to know much – what is discussed in PSHE or Student Support stays there. Teachers just need to know there is something going on. There is an atmosphere of trust between the staff, between the staff and parents, and between the students and teachers.'

'How do you measure that?' reflects Helen. 'You could look at the exam results of the children who have faced the biggest problems. The fact that 96 per cent last year made expected or better than expected progress, and there was no significant difference in the results of vulnerable students when compared to students who don't face the same challenges. The fact that the incidence of bullying is so low. You could look at attendance, which is fantastic. The fact that a student who is facing some of the toughest things at home is here 100 per cent of the time because school is the 100 per cent safe place to be. School should be a haven – not something that makes life more difficult.'

'Some of the older teachers may have been cynical when this started,' says Karen Camp. 'But now – working as a team with us – they're all incredibly supportive. They've seen and felt the difference, not only in terms of girls dealing with problems, and being happier, but also in results. They spend less time handling problems in class, and more time teaching. Less time wondering why students haven't turned up, and more time with a full class who are all engaged in the lesson they've prepared.'

HOW CAN THE CHARITY BEAT (BEATING EATING DISORDERS) HELP YOU?

Fort Pitt had been working with the NSPCC (mentor training) when we visited (see more about the charity's work in Chapter 12) and with the charity Beat.

Beat began life as the Eating Disorders Association (EDA) in 1989 when two local charities, Anorexic Aid and Anorexic Family Aid, merged to form the UK's first national organisation devoted to eating disorders. They were joined by the Society for the Advancement of Research into Anorexia (SARA) in 1992. They are now the world's largest eating disorders charity. Over 1.6 million men and women in the UK are affected by eating disorders. It's a problem that claims more lives that any other mental illness. In any one year the charity can be in contact with hundreds of thousands of individuals, and many more through their website. Their Young Ambassadors are aged between 14 and 25 and speak out about their experiences when they visit schools, helping to reduce the stigma and raise awareness of the impact of eating disorders among students.

For more information visit www.b-eat.co.uk.

IN MY VIEW – JACK JACOBS

'It's my feeling that if teachers took bullying as seriously as attendance, results and behaviour – if there was zero tolerance towards bullying in schools – it wouldn't just help people who are bullied, like me, it would help bullies too.'

JACK JACOBS IS A SUPPORTER OF BEAT, THE CHARITY WORKING TO RAISE AWARENESS OF EATING DISORDERS, AND TO HELP PEOPLE BEAT THEM. JACK HAS RECOVERED FROM ANOREXIA, AND IS TRAINING TO BE AN ACCOUNTANT AT DURHAM UNIVERSITY.

The charity Beat wants to challenge the stigma people with eating disorders face so they can talk about their problems more openly. Beat knows that around 1.6 million people suffer from eating disorders, and a disorder like anorexia stems from low self-esteem and an inability to cope safely with worries and problems. They also know that too many young people develop this problem when they lose weight to try to be happy, or to make people like them more or even notice them less.

I was bullied right through primary and into secondary school for being overweight. Teachers used to try and stop the boys picking on me at primary, but by secondary I'd just got used to it. I acted like it didn't hurt me, but of course I realise now that the more you keep things in, the more it can hurt you later. When I was 14 we moved house, and I decided it would be a fresh start for me and I'd lose weight. I can see now – looking back and knowing what I know – that what I discovered then was something I could control at a time when I couldn't seem to control anything else. I hated being bullied, and blamed myself, and suddenly, when I dieted, I was in charge. It became my life – waking up, walking the dog, controlling what I ate. Even now when things seem out of control it hits me again, that feeling. Anorexia doesn't disappear. You just learn to manage it.

I felt so isolated when my eating disorder developed, and then because I didn't want anyone to know what was happening I isolated myself further. When I was going for treatment at the hospital I used to tell the boys in my class I was going to the dentist. I couldn't tell them the truth. Luckily I could tell my mum, and she supported me throughout.

Anorexia has the highest mortality rate of any psychiatric disorder, from medical complications associated with the illness as well as suicide. Research has found that 20 per cent of anorexia sufferers will die prematurely from their illness. I lost a huge amount of weight in a short time and my heart beat dropped to around 38 beats per minute and I couldn't walk up the stairs. I was so exhausted I'd be asleep before 7. I remember once, in hospital, seeing the nurse's face when she was checking my pulse and I knew it was bad. That I might die. And that was the start of my recovery.

It has been a long few years getting to where I am now, and I wouldn't wish this on anyone else – but I am glad I have been on this journey so I can tell my story, and hopefully help Beat open up this issue so it is discussed in schools and in the media, so children and teenagers can talk about what they are feeling and doing before it really makes them ill. I hope I can contribute to the debate about bullying too. It's my feeling that if teachers took bullying as seriously as attendance, results and behaviour – if there was zero tolerance towards bullying in schools – it wouldn't just help people who are bullied, like me, it would help bullies too. It seems to me that they must have problems, like I did, and their way of taking control of them is to take control of someone else's life and happiness.

12

The ChildLine Workshop

Why It's Time to Let Children Speak Out about Bullying and Abuse

'This is about raising awareness among all children, and all school staff, that the way they treat each other – the culture of their class and their playgrounds – can help empower children so they trust their instincts, build good relationships and seek help when they're in trouble. Or it can do exactly the opposite. It can sometimes silence them forever.'

SHAUN FRIEL, NATIONAL MANAGER, CHILDLINE
SCHOOLS SERVICE, NORTHERN IRELAND

In a primary school hall just outside Belfast, a visitor, Eileen, is putting plastic bricks into a sack. Each brick, she explains to the children in front of her, is a worry. She invites the crowded hall to suggest what worries most children their age have during the day, and bricks representing homework and fall-outs with friends and toothache and forgetting their dinner money and the playground bully and being left out of games and a poorly pet all go into the sack. Then she asks them to imagine carrying this huge load around the school, and to think for a minute how that would get in the way of their day and their PE lesson and playtime and classes, and even eating their lunch.

Then comes the crucial bit. The children have to empty the sack, and to do that they have to find someone to carry the bricks for them – someone to share those worries with. Hands go up, and one by one the bricks come out, children passing them on, they say, to mums, dads, grandmas and granddads, brothers, sisters and friends…

Eileen knows, though, that there will be a few children sitting in the hall today who can't think of anyone quite as quickly as the rest, in or outside school. There may even be a few who just keep quiet and feel their only option is to carry their load out of the hall and with them throughout the day.

This is the NSPCC, and the story gives us a powerful insight into its ChildLine Schools Service in action, today being led by Eileen, one of the charity's volunteers. The charity now has a mission to reach 1.7 million children in 21,000 schools by 2017 with the very simple message that, whatever their worry, they always – *always* – have the right to speak to someone about it, and a right to a life not loaded down with fear and worry. With the aid of its ChildLine mascot Buddy (a huge green speech bubble-shaped character), the NSPCC is running this special national programme to help children understand abuse in all its forms, and to make sure that they are aware that it is wrong for anyone to make a child feel worried or scared. At the same time, the NSPCC aims to open children's eyes to how others in their class may need help unloading their sack. The NSPCC hopes that this message, as part of its larger campaign, can do something about the devastating number of children who are growing up unhappy as a result of bullying, abuse, neglect, or all three.

Hearing every child

The NSPCC launched its new ChildLine Schools Service in 2011 knowing it had to reach more children more quickly and at a younger age. 'We were doing some good work on these issues but knew services like school counselling or peer mentoring, while successful, were only reaching certain numbers of children in certain areas of the country,' says Shaun Friel, national manager of the ChildLine Schools Service in Northern Ireland.

'We were realising that our more universal services like ChildLine were receiving too many calls from children over the age of 12 who were reporting significant trauma over a number of years. Many had waited a long time – too long a time – before they felt they could speak out. What's more, some two-thirds of children who are abused still don't tell anyone, don't feel able to ask for help. We knew absolutely that had to change. It was incumbent on us to do something about it.'

To make this happen the NSPCC is recruiting a national team of intensively trained volunteers like Eileen whose mission is to get into every primary school across the land every two years with a sack of bricks and clear messages about abuse in all its forms – bullying, sexual, emotional, physical – and about every child's right to live free from those things, and crucially, every child's right to speak up and be heard if anything or anyone is making them scared or unhappy.

It can seem like a big and heavy-duty ask for primary schools to make room in their already packed-to-busting school day for talks about abuse. Some schools, says Shaun, believe they're immune to problems, or suggest their students are not ready or able to digest and discuss these issues. Less so these days, though. Not many teachers can deny the harm bullying does anymore, or the prevalence of child abuse. And if teachers have concerns about the content, they are, says Shaun, soon allayed when they look over materials and see how sensitively the issues are handled.

'Society has for some time taught children about road safety, stranger danger and fire safety; we haven't avoided these because it might frighten children every time they cross the road or see a box of matches,' says Shaun. 'Without exception, when schools open up to the idea of this programme and see it in action, they see the value it brings. Many adults admit to making assumptions about how children felt about some of these issues, and about how much they would engage. They are amazed by what they hear, amazed by what they learn from what they hear. Some imagine there will be a hall full of children looking at the ceiling or studying their hands uncomfortably, but what they get is a room full of children with their hands up, wanting to participate and to join the conversation.'

Shaun knows that ChildLine and the NSPCC are, quite rightly, viewed as the charities that tackle child abuse and neglect. But he is keen to stress to schools that this programme is not just about identifying victims of abuse in schools and signposting the help they offer. It is, he says, also about communicating the very explicit message that no child should keep quiet about anything that is scaring them or making them unhappy – and that can be a death in the family, a bully in the playground, or a problem at home.

'Those issues are big enough in themselves. It is not our job to measure concerns, or to tell children what is more significant,' says Shaun. 'But this is about raising awareness among all children, and all school staff, that the way they treat each other – the culture of their class and their playgrounds – can help empower children so they trust their instincts, build good relationships and seek help when they're in trouble. Or it can do exactly the opposite. It can sometimes silence them forever.'

How tackling bullying can change a child's world

Bullying is a prominent issue in these NSPCC workshops and assemblies, and with good reason. 'We know that different schools have different cultures – you sense that when you go in. If that culture is warm, welcoming and caring – a culture where issues like bullying and mutual respect are openly discussed – that makes it easier for children to speak out and ask for help. If not, then of course you risk children going through school feeling it's okay to be laughed at or hurt (via emotional or physical abuse), and that the adults around them will dismiss or ignore the problem, and think they're making a fuss and should toughen up,' says Shaun. 'Then you risk them growing up believing they should persist with relationships which are hurtful and abusive.

'We want fresh messages for these children. We want children to feel rewarded for questioning behaviour they don't feel comfortable with and we want them to be heard. We know – and this is crucial – that if talking works in schools, if children listen to each other, and adults make time for children's concerns, then those same children will feel able to talk again when maybe the worry is more serious, when maybe others are telling them "not to tell",' explains Shaun. 'We know children sometimes test out others – teachers, friends, ChildLine – with smaller worries around the fringes of a bigger issue. They need to know they will be heard and respected before they tell the whole story. That's why it can be so harmful to tell a child that their worry (be it about a single incident in the playground or anxiety at home) isn't important.'

Talking abuse and talking neglect

A few weeks later, Eileen and another volunteer return to the school to work with classes in smaller workshops, and to tackle some of the issues in more detail.

One of the first activities is what they call the 'Okay, Not Okay' session, something that allows them to talk directly about scenarios that may make children feel comfortable/uncomfortable, about things that might happen to them – and it could be physical, emotional or sexual abuse – which they don't feel okay about.

'Central to this is getting children to trust their own feelings about what is right and wrong, and to remind them of their rights to talk about that,' says Shaun Friel. 'We talk about kisses that make them feel loved and comforted, and kisses they might not want to give. Touching that is good and okay and touching they might not be comfortable with.

'The children quickly come up with a whole range of situations where they know touching is okay. Say, when an adult picks them up when they fall, or a nurse holds their hand while they're having an injection, or their parents give them a kiss goodnight, or a cuddle when they're sad,' says Shaun. 'Then they might start to talk about stuff they know isn't okay.

'This exercise isn't about us saying, "that's abuse, but this isn't",' says Shaun. 'While there are those black-and-white scenarios, more often the children who share a concern discuss a grey area where they are confused about what is happening and what they're feeling about it. The exercise is about re-inforcing to children that irrespective of the situation, if they feel uncomfortable, they have a right to talk to someone about that.

'Children have their own barometer of what they feel comfortable with, and the work we do in schools is about getting them to recognise that barometer and trust it and to speak to someone about it when they are uncomfortable or worried. Children in abusive situations have often been groomed by their abuser, and believe there are barriers to getting help (no one will believe you; no one thinks this is wrong; you don't know the words to describe what has happened). That's why it's so important that children's worries are not dismissed, even small ones.

'The sessions are not encouraging children to share personal information with us there and then, though sometimes that happen,' says Shaun. 'It's about encouraging them to recognise they have a right to feel as they do about what's right and wrong, and a right to share those feelings. We're not prescriptive about the people they should contact – the police, social workers, etc. Again, we talk about ChildLine, but we also encourage them to identify who they trust, and who they would talk to if they were worried. Some kids make a list on autopilot: the family network they can confide in, the teachers they respect. Others sit for a while thinking about it.'

In the second part of the workshops, Eileen introduces a student called 'Guy', a story character created by ChildLine to illustrate the issue of neglect, not only so that children can recognise when they are neglected, but also to ensure that the neglected child doesn't become the bullied or isolated child at school.

Eileen shows an animation about Guy and why he is really sad because he gets no food when he gets home, and there is no one to look after him in the evening. He has to get up and get to school without any help from his family. She asks the class how they think Guy may be feeling when he gets to school.

'He might be angry,' says one.

'Or lonely,' says another.

'He might be smelly if he never gets to have a bath,' suggests a boy.

'He could be happy at school compared to how he feels at home…' points out the girl sitting next to him.

'But maybe he's pretending to be happy so no one picks on him,' says her friend.

'Maybe he feels homeless,' says a little boy.

'Homeless?' asks another. 'He has a home.'

'No,' says his classmate. 'He has a house, not a home.'

'We know it's important to distinguish between neglect and poverty,' says Shaun. 'The kids soon recognise that this is not about getting Rice Krispies instead of Coco Pops, or cheap trainers instead of expensive ones; that it is about basic needs not being met. But we know that a lot of children who are neglected at home come into school and get neglected by their friends, too. Because they aren't part of the social group, because of their lack of confidence, even because of the state of the school uniform or their poor attainment in class.'

ChildLine reports that neglect is having an impact on one child in ten in the UK today, and calls to their helpline about neglect have doubled in recent years. And feedback from schools has demonstrated to the ChildLine team that these school workshops have opened up the whole issue of neglect to the school staff, as well as to the children.

'Teachers are telling us they have realised – and subsequently discussed – how if a "Guy" comes from a home where he's neglected and turns up at school and that neglect isn't recognised and he is told off for being late, or forgetting his lunch money, or for looking scruffy, then he's not going to feel their school is a place where he can seek help,' says Shaun. 'They realise the message their "Guy" could get is that what is happening to him, and the way he is being treated, is something that he cannot question or talk about, never mind change.'

So Eileen and the children think about how Guy might seek help. The children turn to their own behaviour first, how they could start to think about not teasing him, or ignoring him, or laughing at his uniform.

'Perhaps,' one says, 'we could have him round to tea.'

'Maybe,' says another, 'we should tell him to get some more help.'

'Maybe,' says a third, 'we could help him do that by actually going with him to speak to a teacher.'

The NSPCC is, with Kidscape, part of the advisory group at the national Anti-Bullying Alliance (see www.anti-bullyingalliance.org.uk). Both charities know it is hard to measure the direct outcomes of their campaigns, and of school programmes like this one. But they are confident they will play a significant part in encouraging children to speak out about what is happening to them. They know that it's here, in schools like this one today, that a child might hear for the first time that what is happening to them is wrong, and feel able to speak up so they can get help putting it right.

'We hope that in years to come we'll hear from schools how educational campaigns like this one have helped change the culture of the class. How they gave children from an early age a sense of how great it is to be kind to each other, and to look out for each other,' says Shaun. 'We hope we'll hear from children and young people who, as a result of what they learned at school, recognised they had rights and asserted them and changed things before it was too late. Maybe we will only really see the difference five or ten years down the line. We're looking for a future where bullying is recognised as unacceptable in every school, and everyone in the school knows they can talk to someone about any abuse they suffer... That has to be a future worth fighting for.'

HOW CAN CHILDLINE AND THE NSPCC HELP YOU?

ChildLine is the UK's free, confidential helpline open all day, every day. It was launched in 1986 by Esther Rantzen, and in 2006 became part of the NSPCC, which added a website (receiving over 2.5 million hits a year, and rising) with information, advice and online tools to give children the confidence to speak out. Children can contact ChildLine by phone on 0800 1111, email or one-to-one chat via the website, www.ChildLine.org.uk

The ChildLine School Services programme is delivered by specially trained volunteers in a way that is accessible, engaging and appropriate for primary school children. All the materials and activities are scripted and have been developed after piloting the service and gaining feedback from children, teachers, parents and education/child protection experts. Schools can check the materials in advance of any visit, and the charity always follows each school's safeguarding procedures.

If you haven't had a visit from ChildLine or would like to volunteer, visit www.nspcc.org.uk/childlineschoolsservice to find out more.

IN MY VIEW – ADE ADEPITAN

'The biggest weakness of human beings is a lack of respect for difference, a lack of empathy for others. The best thing we can do for children is to tackle that.'

ADE ADEPITAN, MBE, PARALYMPIC CHAMPION AND TV
PRESENTER, IS AN AMBASSADOR FOR THE NSPCC.

Supporting the NSPCC is a no-brainer for me. The work they're doing in schools is empowering children to speak up and speak out, for themselves and for others. Speaking up takes courage, so it's so important that when children do, they know they will be heard, and not be ignored, dismissed or laughed at by teachers or the other kids in the school.

I can remember when I was in a mainstream school in London, after we'd moved here from Nigeria. I used to get called 'peg leg', and the kids would take the mickey out of the way I spoke. I was the only child with a disability in the school (my sister, who has Down syndrome, went to a special school), and one of the few black children there. My parents were big on equality and respect, and we'd been taught to treat people as we wanted to be treated and to stand up for others. That gave me confidence and a sense of purpose. When you have that confidence, you don't want to bully, and you don't want to stand by and see others bullied. That has stayed with me.

We know a lot of bullying comes from insecurity and ignorance, from a lack of understanding about differences. That goes beyond colour or disability. There are so many people who are marginalised and isolated and hurt because they are different. The biggest weakness of human beings is a lack of respect for difference, a lack of empathy for others. The best thing we can do for children is to tackle that. Then we can make a real change to the world they're growing up in.

Index